ALL WAYS
COACHING

HOW TO CREATE A
COACHING CULTURE
IN YOUR SCHOOL

Nicholas McKie

First Published 2021
Cadogan Press

© 2021 Nicholas McKie

ISBN: 978-1-8380073-3-1

Set and designed by Cadogan Press
Illustrations by Edd Newson
Printed by Book Printing UK

For
Vicki, Duncan,
Charlotte, Sidney,
Miller and Enid.

About the author

Nicholas McKie is an Associate Professor and Professional Certified Coach with the International Coaching Federation (ICF), working with individuals, teams and organisations all over the world to unlock their leadership potential and enhance the quality of educational practice. The Founder and Director of Persyou, Nicholas specialises in executive leadership coaching and development with leaders across the education sector and beyond.

Nicholas's career path has been rich and diverse, starting as a professional musician before entering teaching in the UK and then internationally, rising to School Principal and UK School Inspector. He has worked in schools in Japan, Egypt, China and the US as well as in the UK working in both state and independent sectors. His experience gives him a unique perspective on leadership in a range of settings, which he has pursued through his coaching work.

Nicholas combines coaching and leadership development with his role as an Associate Professor at the University of Warwick, UK. With his wealth of overseas teaching experience, Nicholas leads on international education programmes, having developed and established Warwick's inaugural PGCE international course as well as lecturing on the local PGCE programme. Nicholas's popular podcast, *Persyou Inspiring Leadership* continues to bring engaging stories, insight and expertise from across the world of educational leadership.

Persyou provides:

- Executive coaching for school leaders
- Group and team coaching programmes
- Training on how to create a school wide coaching culture
- Coaching and leadership training
- International teacher training

For further information please contact Nicholas: hello@persyou.com
www.persyou.com

Praise for All Ways Coaching

In this thought-provoking book, Nicholas has pulled together a huge range of international research and combined it with his own extensive experience to produce a comprehensive and optimistic review of what makes great coaching in schools. A must-read.

Dame Alison Peacock, CEO - Chartered College of Teaching

All Ways Coaching is an authentic and informed resource on a growing area in education, from a sector leading coach. Nicholas' book compliments his superb skills as a coach, shaping leadership and coaching in schools across the world.

Chris Seal, Principal, Shrewsbury International School, Bangkok and FOBISIA Committee Member.

I knew immediately that anything Nicholas would write on the subject of coaching would be good and it is. Thoughtful, practical, and well evidenced. Do read it.

Professor Deborah Eyre, Founder and Chair, High Performance Learning

In this superb review of the relevant research, combined with his own significant experience, Nicholas brings to life how a coaching approach can transform so many important areas in the working life of teachers and school leaders in any setting, including those in an international context. Highly recommended."

Ann Haydon, Head - Harrow International School Hong Kong

All Ways Coaching' is the essential guide, manual and reference book to introduce a coaching culture in your school. Clear, comprehensive and concise, it helps you to navigate the extensive world of coaching with ease. Having read 'All Ways Coaching' I am now better informed, more confidently equipped and empowered with a professional language to introduce a coaching culture in my school.

Kai Vacher, Principal, British School, Muscat, Oman

Anyone in a leadership role, privileged enough to coach those in education, or aspiring to either of those things, would benefit from reading this book. Designed to build your knowledge and understanding of coaching in an educational setting chapter by chapter, it caters for those with a range of experience levels and offers something new to those who have been coaching others for some time.

Dr Victoria Carr, Head teacher, Woodlands Primary School, UK

I enjoyed All Ways Coaching because of its clarity, timeliness and relevance. The steps necessary to establish a coaching culture were delineated with a clear explanation of each domain. I particularly liked the way that research and strategies were integrated making it easy to see the connections. I would readily recommend the book to anyone looking for a reference guide on how to deploy coaching techniques for the wider benefit of the school.

Brian Cooklin, Managing Director, India, Nord Anglia Education

This is a brilliant book for leaders and stakeholders in any school. Coaching plays a big role in developing teamwork. After reading this book, school leaders will understand the importance and significance of coaching. A must read!

Anuradha Monga, Founder and Chairperson at The Association of International Schools of India

Nicholas has written the definitive guide on coaching. It's a must read - very accessible, concise and gets to the point. There are plenty of useful strategies to help you understand and create a coaching culture in your own setting. Highly recommended!
Irfan Latif, Principal DLD College London

Nicholas has written an insightful, well informed and beautifully articulated book on the profession of coaching. He challenges conventional approaches and pulls the reader into his tried and tested approach with much eloquence and ease. It is an enjoyable read and will provoke many to rethink their approach to coaching and will encourage others to explore engaging a coach.

Rene Carayol, MBE, Executive coach and author of Spike.

All Ways Coaching is an incredibly useful resource for both aspiring coaches and those with mentoring/coaching experience who wish to hone their skills and further develop their expertise. From an Initial Teacher Education perspective, this book supports a necessary shift from mentoring to coaching and will prove invaluable for university and school mentors in their role as 'expert colleague'.

Julie Taylor, Primary School Direct and Primary Mentor Lead, University of Warwick, UK.

This is an excellent coaching guide for school leaders. I wish I had access to this when embarking on my leadership journey.

John Gwyn Jones MBE, CEO of the Federation of British International Schools in Asia (FOBISIA).

As an educational leader All Ways Coaching gives me a nice, accessible overview of the main models and theories used in coaching and the key skills that are necessary. If I was looking to start introducing coaching into my college this would be a great foundation.
Emma Wilkinson, Vice-Principal, CATS College Canterbury, UK

All Ways Coaching is an apt title. In working with Nick, it is clear that he is, indeed, all ways coaching - and in all sorts of ways. Coaching methodologies are embedded in Nick's leadership practice, his work with university students, and in his support of fellow professionals. This approach, and Nick's experiences, are neatly distilled within these pages. If you'd like to embed coaching into your daily practice, the book will make an ideal coaching partner.

Dr Denry Machin, Co-Author of 'International Schooling: The Teacher's Guide'

Contents

Foreword

All Ways Coaching is a very timely book. There is a growing recognition from across the global education sector that how we support colleagues to develop and grow is fundamental to the success of any school or wider system. The contribution that high quality coaching can make for teachers and school leaders, enacted within the right culture and climate, can ultimately make a significant difference to the lives of the children and young people we serve.

Whilst there is a real sense that coaching is 'coming of age' within education, there is nonetheless a real risk that, as with other developments, the way our profession implements a coaching approach fails to capitalise on the benefits it offers. In this impressive book, Nicholas McKie has created a research-informed approach to the implementation of coaching that draws on his own extensive experience, thoughtfully examining the intersections between coaching, teaching and leadership in a way that gives schools an accessible and thought-provoking overview of how to harness the benefits that coaching can bring to every facet of school life.

Rich in powerful coaching theory and its practical application demonstrated through an impressive range of case-studies, this refreshing summary of the key elements to consider when investing in coaching will be an invaluable guide for school leaders and other practitioners reflecting on both their own personal development as coaches as well as how to successfully implement a coaching approach within their own school.

Andy Buck
Founder of Leadership Matters
Creator of the BASIC Coaching Method

Introduction

My first teaching experiences were to be found while enjoying sport or playing music. I was constantly looking for areas where I was confident in my playing and trying to ensure that these were expressed well. I was also identifying areas of weakness, perhaps a kick or stroke that I couldn't master or perhaps a musical scale that I couldn't quite nail down. I invented study techniques and practices to help me develop my ability to play in certain ways. I was taking responsibility for my own development and essentially teaching myself.

My first formal teaching experience was at Music College in London, where I had the opportunity to run workshop-based activities for groups of children across a range of ages in the London borough of Harrow. It was an informal environment, promoting creativity with opportunities for students to be exposed to more contemporary and diverse musical styles. Explanatory dialogue was kept to a minimum and time was spent practicing different calls and rhythmic patterns on a range of instruments. In many ways this wasn't formal music teaching, but rather allowing the students the freedom to connect to a wider context.

Before the world of education and coaching its leaders became my passion, I was a professional bassoon player, part of the woodwind section in an orchestra. After embarking on my professional performing career, subsequent teaching opportunities came about in Mumbai whilst I was playing in the Bombay Chamber Orchestra. Although a completely different setting to the Harrow schools the same informal teaching approaches were successful, despite some language barriers and cultural differences. It was the same when I went on to teach English in Japan – the most successful teaching and learning took place when I adopted an informal approach, sensitive to the students with an awareness of social context and community.

Later, while undertaking formal teacher training in the UK, I realised that my previous experience had been a wonderful playground that had allowed me to experiment with different kinds of pedagogy and, although I did not know it then, I had been incorporating core coaching skills throughout.

Through formal teacher training I came to understand the importance and necessity of traditional teaching approaches but throughout my teaching career – whether in UK state or independent schools, overseas in both international and local settings – the principle of combining formal and informal teaching approaches remained. This continues to inform my coaching and teacher training work.

All Ways Coaching places a focus at the intersection of coaching, teaching and leading.

Striking a chord

Being part of an orchestra is a great education in how individuals and teams operate and perform, both collectively and individually. There are few better examples of team working than an orchestral performance. The contribution of every member of the orchestra, and of every 'team' or section within it is vital to the final result. A leader in an effective organisation will be like the second bassoonist at times: critical but not always playing the melody, out of the limelight but laying the foundation for success.

At other times leaders will need to be out in front playing the main melody, perhaps a solo part or in tandem with another section principal. Sometimes they will make mistakes but that comes with the territory when playing a solo part under pressure: the key is to be able to put it behind you and move on.

As an education leader you must appreciate the roles within teams, understand expectations and know when to focus on the micro or macro and when 'active listening' is important across the group. The idea of creating synergy across differing facets of an organisation, learning from each other and mirroring good practice in order to create a finished performance is crucial. In an orchestra, everyone is a leader, whether a first or second bassoonist, trumpet player or first violin. Responsibility is distributed within a high trust environment with all members sharing in both success and failure.

I have had the good fortune to play at a professional level for world-class orchestras, and to appreciate their teamwork and leadership strengths at first hand. This knowledge helped me enormously when progressing from teacher to School Principal and I still incorporate this thinking within my work, both in my university role as an Associate Professor and as a Certified Professional Coach.

As teachers and educational leaders, we need to be all ways coaching. I hope my insights will strike a chord with you too.

A word about the definition of coaching

Coaching has influences from many spheres, including self-help, psychology, psychotherapy, spirituality, business, sport and cognitive behaviour. Coaching can be scientific but also has a lot of similarities to creating art: the process, ingredients, improvisation, timing, an audience as well as the critics!

Definitions are provided in each section of Part 1 to provide you with an understanding of the different coaching domains I explore in the book. Coaching courses certified by governing bodies such as the International Coaching Federation (ICF) and the European Mentoring and Coaching Council (EMCC) are another useful starting point to ignite your coaching journey and can evidence your coaching competency as you progress.

Using the book

Drawing on my experiences of teaching, leading and coaching all over the world, my hope is that this book will illustrate, contextualise and illuminate a fresh perspective on how to deploy and use coaching in your setting, as well as supporting you with creating a coaching culture in your school.

The book is split into four parts:

Part 1: Your coaching evolution
Part 2: A coaching way of teaching
Part 3: A coaching way of leading
Part 4: Case studies

In Part 1 we explore your coaching evolution, taking you through three ways of coaching, or domains, which support the creation of a coaching culture:

- Fundamental
- Systemic
- Transformative

In Part 2 we draw on Part 1 to outline a coaching way of teaching framed around three teaching approaches:

- Formal
- Non-formal
- Informal

In Part 3 we draw on previous chapters to outline how to implement a coaching way of leading framed around:

- Awareness
- Relationships
- Agility

The book is designed to build your knowledge and understanding of coaching in an educational setting chapter by chapter.

Therefore, I would invite you to read Part 1 first in order to understand the main coaching themes before applying this to the subsequent sections on teaching and leadership. My hope is that what you will take away from reading this book can enhance your service to the people you work with, by helping you to place coaching at the heart of education. I also hope your coaching journey is one of pleasure and enjoyment as you yourself learn, develop and grow.

Part One

Your Coaching Evolution

The embryonic stages of my coaching practice were focussed on what I was engaged with. Had I incorporated all the coaching skills? Had I followed the coaching model correctly? Did my client have a life-changing epiphany? As I progressed and grew more experienced and comfortable with coaching, the spotlight shifted away from me as coach and onto my coachee's agenda. It was all about the person I was working with in a more nuanced non-directive way. The more I coached the more I realised the importance of the context both myself and my clients were working in.

Even within a one-to-one coaching conversation a variety of working and personal contexts can come into play. Throughout my coaching assignments I began to engage with the people around my client a lot more, seeing them as key players in the coaching partnership. For example, when working with a senior leader it was important to glean feedback from a range of stakeholders across the school or group they were working in as well as factoring in their personal landscape. When coaching teachers, the relevance of contact with parents as well as students and staff had to be taken into consideration.

My previous experience has taught me that, in schools, we see change emerging through multiple microsystems and teams. As my coaching experience, training and practice grew so my assumptions were challenged further. I found my coaching skills were not the only area where I was developing; the coaching process itself began to take a back seat as deeper themes began to emerge. It is through all these experiences I have formulated a blueprint for a coaching evolution culminating in a coaching culture.

Part 1 of this book offers a route map for coaching evolution through three domains:

- Fundamental
- Systemic
- Transformative

The domains each have subdomains as illustrated on the diagram below.

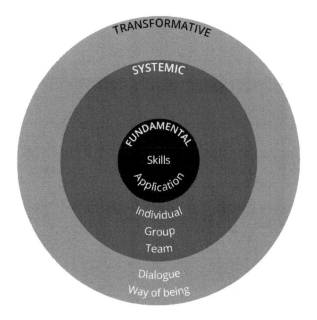

Chapters 1 to 3 outline each domain, their subdomains, definition and approach. The domains, whilst not a necessarily a progression, can be used to provide you with a coaching evolution. They will also help you develop your coaching repertoire, both in educational contexts and beyond. The progression along the domains is nuanced and you will see some cross over between them. All domains are valid and of value.

The domains explored in Part 1 also demonstrate a clear pathway for leaders to embed a coaching culture in an educational and indeed organisational context. This is explored in Chapter 4.

Remember that there is no requirement to progress through the domains; for some of you it will be appropriate to simply focus on the fundamentals and look for ways to embed these into your classroom or general interactions across your setting. For others this evolution will progress to full coaching culture. My hope is that you will adapt according to your context.

Throughout the book I will refer to those being coached as coachees – whoever you are working with within your specific setting.

Part One: Chapter 1

The Fundamental Domain

Fundamental coaching definition:

A one-to-one conversation that focusses on the enhancement of learning and development through increasing self-awareness and a sense of personal responsibility, where the coach facilitates the self-directed learning of the coachee through questioning, active listening, and appropriate challenge in a supportive and encouraging climate.[1]

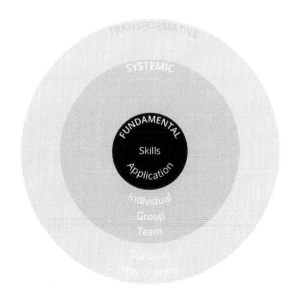

The Fundamental domain is the first step on the coaching ladder and I have found it the most widely used and well known approach across the education sector. It is concerned with the basic skills, processes and models of coaching in a one-to-one coaching relationship. A typical coaching interaction in this domain will take place in a work environment, whether office or classroom at school. In this domain you will learn to progress from 'inheritor' of skills to 'enactor' of coaching, or to put it another way; move from focussing on yourself to focussing on the coachee. By adopting the Fundamental coaching approach you will:

- be able to support the coachee by defining goals
- come up with solutions and hold the coachee accountable
- help people think through things and come up with the answers themselves[2]

Firstly, you need to be aware of two potentially conflicting standpoints:

- The belief that the client has all the answers (coaching)
- The belief that the coach has the answers (mentoring)

Within a directive (mentoring) coaching style, you will be more likely to solve problems *for* the coachee, whereas in a non-directive (coaching) approach you will help the person to find their own solutions[3].

In the Fundamental domain your focus as coach is on being non-directive and non-judgmental. You must strive to avoid deciding what is best for your coachee. Educators are generally used to teaching and delivering information, so don't worry that you may find being non-directive tricky to begin with, this is perfectly natural!

Skills and Application

The Fundamental domain is split into two sub domains:

- skills
- application

The first, skills, is focused on you as a coach, developing your own coaching skills and awareness. The second, application, shifts the focus from yourself to the coachee – you will start to apply the coaching skills.

Coaching Skills

Core Fundamental coaching techniques cover the seven coaching skills shown in the diagram below, underpinned by 'holding' which we will now explore.

Holding

'Holding', is a space where your colleagues (for example) feel confident enough to engage in coaching and allow you to apply your coaching skills.

The first skill to understand is that in a coaching relationship you have a responsibility to hold the coachee's agenda, not yours. This might require you to help your coachee focus on what they really want without your influence. We will explore this further later in the Systemic and Transformative domains but alongside holding the coachee's agenda this is also about the person you are working with feeling that they are in a safe pair of hands. Key holding skills are being welcoming through verbal and non-verbal behaviour as well as being interested and encouraging. For example, nodding your head and maintaining eye contact.

Implementing aspects of holding skills can be difficult depending on your relationship with the coachee, for example, if you are in a management or leadership role in relation to them. The default tendency for many of us is to instruct someone less experienced and go into broadcaster mode. Simply asking a question and getting others' opinions rather than first giving yours can be extremely powerful. Trust is essential here as well as self-restraint, to fully 'hold' the space to allow conversations to flow and develop impactful coaching.

Listening

It may sound obvious, but listening is a core coaching skill that allows you to get a sense of a person's context and situation. Good listening also has the effect of fostering trust in a relationship. There are many ways to explain types of listening. I find iPEC coaching's[4] three different levels of listening are easy to digest and understand:

- subjective
- objective
- Intuitive

Subjective

Subjective listening can be described as everyday listening – content is heard through how it relates to the listener. Subjective listening is therefore based not on the context of the person speaking, but through the lens and agenda of the listener themselves. This inevitably makes for a different interpretation of what is being said. Countertransference, whereby the listener treats the person as someone they know and who is directly involved in their life can also occur. This can make you lose objectivity and venture into the kind of friend relationship where you would be giving advice.

Example:

Teacher: I had the worst lesson observation this morning.

Colleague: We have all been through it. I always just go through the motions and wait for the feedback.

Objective

Objective listening takes places when the listener is solely focussed on the other person. There is no attempt to create a personal connection or how the content relates to the listener and their own context. Objective listening can be effective in beginning to understand the other person (the coachee) and their situation.

Example:

Teacher: I had the worst lesson observation this morning.

Colleague: It sounds tough, but you got through it. Congratulations!

Intuitive

Intuitive listening is concerned with the listener giving their full attention, to be able to hone-in to *all* of the sensory components of the conversation and to connect with the real message. In some cases, the coach can pick up a sense, a feeling or thought that the coachee may not be fully aware of[5]. This will involve:

- tone of voice
- feelings
- body language
- maintaining eye contact

- listening for what is *not* potentially being verbalised

Example:

Teacher: I had the worst lesson observation this morning.

Colleague: It sounds like you got through an observation which you found challenging and maybe even a little bit frustrating.

Progressing listening

A more in-depth (and therefore more useful) listening model is framed around four progressive stages:

- noise: listening for the chance to speak
- content: listening for the words spoken
- intention: listening for what others want to say
- identity: listening for who other people are[6]

In my experience most of us spend the majority of our time in the 'noise' and 'content' stages; we listen with the purpose of getting our point across as soon as possible and construct our own meaning from what is being said. I can certainly recollect many times when I jumped in to have my say in meetings, trying to push my own agenda! This approach can be beneficial to us – especially in times of turbulence and chaos when quick decisions need to be made – but is not suitable for a coaching situation.

When listening with 'intention', we are trying to hone-in on what others are really trying to say, perhaps seeking clarification, paraphrasing and summarising what is being said.

When we want to understand not only what is being said, but why people are trying to say it, we are listening for 'identity', a form of listening that helps us truly understand the other person and how best to relate with them moving forward.

In these stages you also tune into your coachee's non-verbal behaviour such as breathing and posture. I found this deeper listening really useful when working overseas due to the language barrier making conversations difficult at times. You can decipher a lot about someone's emotions from their body language which can then support subsequent questioning.

Developing people and fostering positive relationships necessitates more time spent in the 'intention' and 'identity' stages. We will explore these further in Chapters 2 and 3.

Questioning

Questions are a core Fundamental coaching skill and key to creating the right environment for effective coaching conversations[7]. Questions need to be:

- empowering
- open-ended
- clarity seeking
- probing
- challenging
- thought-provoking
- future directed
- solution orientated

Good use of questions will cause a person to search for new possibilities and answers. In *The Art of Powerful Questions*[8] the architecture of powerful questions is explored through three dimensions:

- construction
- scope
- assumptions

Question construction

Asking closed questions saves people from having to think. But an open question necessitates them to think for themselves and consider their response[9].

By simply changing the interrogative we can open up the possibility of more valuable and deep inquiry.

Example:

Closed question:

- Are you happy with our departmental meetings?

Open questions:

- *When* have you been most happy with our departmental meetings?

- *What* is it about our departmental meetings that you find most useful?

- *How* do you think we can develop our departmental meetings?

- *Why* might it be that our departmental meetings haven't been as successful as we would like?

Question scope

In order to make questioning effective we need to be aware of the scope of the dialogue and conversational context. By asking questions that are too small in scope we can inhibit answers. By stretching our questioning too wide we can be asking too much of people, extending beyond areas that they can effectively action within their control or remit. Gradually scaling the scope of questioning is a better approach.

Example:

- What is the best way to manage our department?
- What is the best way to manage our school?
- What is the best way to manage our education system?

Ask yourself how your question is enabling someone to attain their goal or solution in their current context, and scale or adapt accordingly.

Scaling questions

These can be very helpful in understanding a current situation and igniting dialogue on how to create improvement and change.

Example:

Coach: On a scale of 1-10 where, with 10 being 'my performance is excellent' and 1 being 'my performance is awful', do you currently sit?

Coachee answers: 6

Coach: What makes you say that?

Coach: OK, so what would an 8 look like to you?

Coach: Then what would be a first step in moving up to an 8?

Question types to avoid

Certain questions are to be avoided if you are looking for more fully engaged and effective dialogue.

Question assumptions

It is important to understand that we can potentially lead a person to a specific – and possibly incorrect – conclusion by the way we pose questions.

This is called suggestive insinuation and occurs when your own assumptions enter the interaction and cause you to ask a leading question or presume there are certain beliefs present in the person you are coaching.

Example:

Do you have any issues with the School Principal?

The form of this question insinuates that the coachee has a potential issue with the School Principal.

Transforming this into a more open-ended question that is not framed around an assumption offers scope to explore any issues more fully.

What is your relationship with the School Principal like?

Leading questions

A leading question is a question that presumes and influences the answer.

Example:

You find the deputy head difficult to work with as well, don't you?

Multiple questions

Multiple questions involve layering queries within one question. This type of question confuses what you are actually asking and may result in your coachee only satisfactorily answering one aspect, or the aspect they find the easiest to answer.

Example:

How do think the lesson went? Did the students meet the objectives? What feedback do you think you will get? How long until your next observation?

Next time you listen to an interview on the radio or television see if you notice how many times multiple questions are asked. You will be surprised!

Seven questions to get you started

Another sound and accessible starting point for questions is found in Michael Bungay Stanier's excellent *The Coaching Habit*[10] in which seven questions are outlined:

- The kick start question: what's on your mind?
- The awe question: and what else?
- The focus question: what's the real challenge here for you?
- The foundation question: what do you want?
- The lazy question: how can I help?
- The strategic question: if you are saying yes to this, what are you saying no to?
- The learning question: what was the most useful for you?

The awe question can be of particular use in drilling down into themes and issues and is a good conversation opener. By asking 'what else?' you give the impression there is something else you are searching for without leading the coachee down any specific theme. This is a question I use a lot and works very well when conversations are proving difficult to develop. This also applies to teaching contexts as well. The focus question is also an effective tool to begin to understand what the personal challenge is for your coachee, rather than simply the context around it. Simply adding 'for you' makes this more personal which in turn can get to the bottom of issues and accelerate the change process.

An example that springs to mind was when coaching a Headteacher in the UK who was taking one year's sabbatical. When I initially asked, 'what's the real challenge here?' they told me about all the meetings they had to facilitate and handover, including introducing the interim Head to parents and governors. This was of course important but nothing that my coachee couldn't handle efficiently. These were the surface issues. When I asked, 'what's the real challenge here for you in this transition?', the conversation completely changed. This was about the anxiety of letting go of a school that they had developed and the fear of losing their identity. These were the deeper issues that weren't being addressed by the opening question.

At times you may have to ask the focus question more than once to enable your coachee to open up to deeper reflections, but this can be very powerful.

Paraphrasing and summarising

Paraphrasing refers to presenting existing information using a different form but similar number of words, which conveys the same meaning.

Summarising is different in that the message is based in the original themes but incorporating *fewer* words[11]. When effective paraphrasing and summarising accompany 'intention' and 'identity' listening you are demonstrating good coach engagement and understanding of the coachee which will in turn enable you to move through issues more easily.

Example:

Coachee: Sometimes it feels like the entire class just do not listen to a word I say and I get no support from my department.

Coach (paraphrasing): It sounds like you are having difficulties with your class which is not being helped by your department?

Coach (summarising): So, what I am hearing you say is no one is listening to you at present?

Empathising

In general educators are used to being empathic. We tend to want people to learn and develop and part of this is knowing what makes them tick. In coaching it is particularly important to be able to see the world through the eyes of another person and so connect with them in a non-judgmental way. Empathy engenders trust and understanding which in turn will help to foster an effective coaching relationship.

Example:

Coachee: I have been working on my school reports all over the weekend, I didn't even have chance to spend any time with my children.

Coach: I would imagine it would be frustrating to have to take work home at the weekend, especially missing out on time with your children. That must be really difficult for you.

Clarifying

When speaking with someone you need to be sure that you fully understand what they are trying to communicate. A clarifying approach can help you better identify specific information being put forward. Only then are you (as the coach) able to fully explore the issues.

Example:

Coachee: I am trying to create a more positive culture in the school.

Coach: What exactly do you mean by 'positive culture'?

Tip:

Don't be put off if you find yourself clarifying a lot particularly in initial coaching sessions. You could frame this by telling your coachee:

'You may notice that I will ask you to clarify quite a few things in the session today. This is completely normal. It just lets me understand what your challenges are.'

Acknowledging

When you acknowledge what another person says you are demonstrating that you have actively been listening to them. Acknowledgement is then a powerful form of communication.

This is different from summarising or paraphrasing in that you are not necessary trying to relay information, more letting people know you have heard them.

Example:

Coachee: I have been trying to get along with the senior leadership team, but whatever I do we just do not click.

Coach: So, it sounds as if you are really putting the effort in to create positive relationships but not getting the results you want?

Forwarding the action

This skill is focused around getting someone to move forward through the setting of goals. In one respect it is about inspiring your coachee to new levels of action and engagement by seeing the best in them.

It is also about goal setting. Setting specific and challenging goals increases enthusiasm, with more important goals leading to the production of greater engagement than less important goals[12].

The Fundamental domain draws on a traditional goal-setting approach. This type of goal setting has positive effects when:

- the task is straightforward
- the task is routine

- the person believes they have the competence and self-efficacy to achieve the task
- they are looking to improve their performance[13]

The diagram below outlines a typical goal setting process[14]. You will see that this process begins with identifying an issue before setting a goal and developing action plans to achieve it.

Once you act you then monitor your progress and potentially tweak or change your approach to finally attain success.

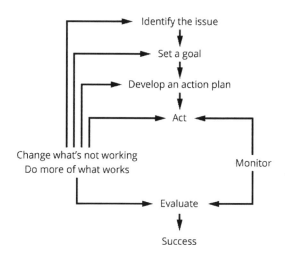

Example:

Let's take a lack of communication as an example issue. The goal could be ensuring that the weekly staff meeting minutes are disseminated to all staff. The action plan would then specify who would take the minutes on a rota, who would be responsible for emailing these to all staff and when these would be sent. A monitoring period would include feedback from staff as to the consistency of this communication. Tweaks need to be made in light of the feedback before a successful routine is put into practice.

Goal-setting tool

The 'AIM SMART' process[15] can also be a sound traditional goal setting tool to accompany the above process.

Firstly, the coach helps the coachee to identify and set an appropriate goal:

> **A**cceptable – what is the minimum you can do?
> **I**deal – what is the maximum you can do?
> **M**iddle – what is a realistic middle ground?

Once you have clarified your goal you can follow the 'SMART' process to track your progress:

- **S**pecific – What is the first step towards your goal?
- **M**easurable – What does success look like in terms of your 'specific' first step?
- **A**chievable – Is the first step possible?
- **R**easonable – How reasonable are your actions? Can you get it done?
- **T**ime – by when will you complete the first step of your goal?

If, during the SMART process, it is clear that the goal is not attainable for whatever reason, simply revisit the AIM stage to further clarify the overarching goal, before once again progressing through the SMART stage. This process is a great one to use with staff as part of appraisals as well as setting targets with students.

The key is to spend sufficient time in the AIM stage because once you have agreed the goal things tend to run more smoothly. This stage may be a little messy but allow enough time to jostle with ideas before settling on a goal.

Setting courageous goals

Although focused, at times the traditional SMART approach above can be limiting. Setting courageous goals can support more aspirational thinking. For example:

- We will increase the percentage of students achieving higher grades by 5% in the next academic year (SMART target)

or

- Over the next academic year we will achieve our best results ever across all grades (courageous targets)

As a coach you can help people move towards more courageous targets by following the process:

- dream
- share
- start[16]

Dream

Encourage your coachee to think beyond the current restraints of their situation by asking:

- "If you believed that anything is possible, what would you want to achieve?"

Share

Sharing a goal can help get buy in and support commitment to achieving the goal itself. Ask:

- "If you were at your most courageous, who else would you share this goal with?"

Start

This is about you supporting your coachee to get things moving towards their goal. Ask:

- "What is the smallest tangible step you could make next week towards this goal?"

Example:

I frequently use this process with trainee teachers internationally. The 'dream' stage gets responses such as, 'I really want this difficult class to listen to what I say.' We can then develop this into something along the lines of 'I want to feel like a confident teacher by the end of the first term.' We might then get them to tell not just their subject mentor but maybe their professional mentor (who is usually a senior leader in the school). This then ups the ante a little. A first tangible step could be observing other teachers to identify teaching skills to incorporate into their own practice, before then being observed in their own teaching.

The importance of vision to your goal setting

Vision can be described as how you want things to be in the future and is a key component of forwarding the action. I find that the clearer the vision the more buy in and motivation increases. I like to focus on what it will look like when the goal has been achieved. For example, the setting, what you are wearing, the smells, the details that will make the vision as real as possible.

In education a lot of time is spent creating text-heavy action plans, whether through lesson planning, school improvement plans and performance management or inspection. I have always felt for a sector with differentiation and adaptation at the heart of its philosophy, this mindset is not always adopted when working with each other. The same can be said in terms of coaching, with coachees frequently asked to write down goals and highly involved action plans.

There is an alternative way to making goal setting more tangible for both coach and coachee that combines both visuals and text. I have found this can work well with coachees and really helps to articulate vision. It is called Polaris[17] after the North Star, reflecting its purpose as something to guide you on your journey through change. Polaris is a three-stage process:

i. The coachee chooses an image that relates to the coaching challenge and which ideally stimulates positive emotions (e.g., inspiration, excitement).

ii. The coachee decides upon a headline that concisely captures their overall purpose.

iii. Below the headline are three to five 'cognitive reminders' – short bullet points that identify key behaviours, values or phrases that are meaningful in the coachee's pursuit of the goal[18].

Example:

I worked with a school principal on how to handle the demands of running a large international school in the Far East. Challenges were centred around the building of a new campus at the same time as managing three schools of differing age ranges during a global pandemic.

i *Choosing the image*
Firstly, we discussed the context of their current situation. I asked the question, 'What image would you choose to describe the challenges in front of you?'

The image they chose was of a climber slowly ascending a mountain. The mountain symbolised the current challenges (steepness) and opportunities (pioneering) they were encountering.

ii. *Choosing the headline*
Secondly, we discussed the overarching theme of the goal. This was explored through questioning the current approach, philosophy and utilisation of strengths. The idea of taking things **one step at a time** resonated.

iii. *Three to five 'cognitive reminders'*
Thirdly, we explored what they had to do in order to keep moving up the mountain.

- It was important to them that they remained strategic in how they navigated uncertain times (**critical thought**).
- There was no point ruminating and fighting things beyond his control (**control the controllable**).

- The importance of remaining true to themselves in the way they 'turned up' at work and beyond. This encapsulated both their way of working and relationships (**embrace who you are**).

The coachee decided upon this image to encapsulate their vision (below). This became their Polaris – it was referred to in coaching sessions and also as a point of reference outside of our sessions.

They used the image as their screensaver, a useful and constant reminder of their overarching vision and direction of travel.

One step at a time
Critical thought
Control the controllables
Embrace who you are

Energy in a Coaching Context

Often, the very first step in the application of coaching skills is in recognising the obstacles that are preventing your coachee from moving forward. Only then can you coach them through those obstacles effectively. It is only by investigating the factors that influence how someone 'turns up' and reacts to various events and circumstances, that allows the deeper exploration of what prevents people from operating at higher energy levels, what's holding them back from accessing opportunities in life or connecting to their passion.

Enormous amounts have been written about 'energetic work' in terms of self-healing, aura, connections and intuition. Energy in this sense could be described as "an unseen power that connects all things, how we express our emotions, make contact, fulfil commitments and live out our roles"[19]. The most common energies in this realm are usually 'Ki' (Japanese) and 'Chi' or 'Qi' (Chinese) and 'Prana' (Indian)[20].

'Ki' for example can best be described as a 'life force energy'. When your 'Ki' is flowing freely you feel healthy, free and strong. If your 'Ki' is low then this manifests as tiredness, weakness and lethargy[21]. In the teaching world, consider how often you feel tired and run down at the end of term, only to become ill in the holidays because your energy levels are low!

In my coaching practice I refer to *Energy Leadership* by Bruce Schneider[22]. Schneider provides an explanation around how people operate in terms of different types of energy and the advantages and disadvantages of resonating in differing energetic levels. Essentially, he demonstrates that there are two main types of energy:

- anabolic
- catabolic

Anabolic energy

This is a high resonating energy, which is constructive, healing and focused around growth. In essence this energy allows you to move forward and achieve positive success and results not just in the short term but longer term too. Tapping into this high frequency energy allows you to embrace what is around you with more awareness, freedom, creativity and joy.

Anabolic energy is associated with connection to everyone and everything, being highly conscious and fearless. This doesn't mean things always go to plan, but you react in a way that is developmental and positive.

Catabolic energy

This is described as a heavier, dense energy. This low frequency energy drains your resources, can be destructive and limits your ability to see all the choices available to you. It is associated with being the victim, fighting your way through life with a perceived lack of options. Resonating in catabolic energy for sustained periods can affect your physical and mental health and impact on those around you.

Energetic presentation

The amount of overall anabolic and catabolic energy we each possess and have available at any given time is called our Energetic Presentation. Everyone has a unique combination of energy, which shows up in various situations, for different periods of time and is determined by our feelings, beliefs, thoughts and behaviours. It is important to note that there is no right, wrong, good or bad in terms of where you currently resonate, as there are advantages and disadvantages to operating at every level. For example, at lower catabolic energy levels, conflict, anger and defiance can enable you to cope and get a lot done, both in terms of motivating yourself and others. This is essential at certain times in our lives. However, over time, these behaviours can also alienate people who do not respond well to forcefulness and anger.

Individuals will resonate at different energetic levels depending on the circumstances, but it is the time that you spend in the lower level catabolic states before you turn the energy into action that is the key. People who resonate in the higher anabolic energy levels are able to use the lower levels consciously dependent on what serves them best in a particular situation.

This entails being both an observer and participant at the same time. Crucially, remember that energy is a constant, it cannot be destroyed, it is all around us – the aim is to gain the ability to decide where energy is focussed, to harness it in a positive way in alignment with our goals.

Your overall energy level therefore, is a strong indicator of success in various aspects of life. Studies prove that higher resonating levels of energy are associated with higher levels of satisfaction in terms of relationships, personal development and achievement. In essence, increasing your anabolic energy will enable you to perform better.

So, what exactly stops us from accessing this positive energy more often?

Energy blocks

There can be seen to be four major inner energy blocks that may be preventing your energy resonating at higher anabolic levels. These blocks could be holding you back from achieving the things you want as well as the people you coach and the students you teach. In my coaching training in the US through iPEC coaching[23] we referred to these blocks as GAIL:

- **G**remlins
- **A**ssumptions
- **I**nterpretations
- **L**imiting beliefs

Awareness of these blocks can allow you to utilise your fundamental questioning skills to challenge and open up your coachee's capacity to move forward.
In terms of order, it is best to start with limiting beliefs and work up as these are the easiest to identify and work through.

Limiting beliefs

These beliefs or conclusions about ourselves or the world that inhibits, limits or constrains us in a particular way. For example, a common limiting belief I hear from school leaders is around public speaking, where this might take place in front of peers.

There is generally no evidence to support the belief. Your role as a coach is to challenge thinking and disrupt such beliefs.

Example:

Coachee: My assemblies are terrible. I am just not good at public speaking.

Coach: Where did you get that idea from?
or
How true is that belief?
or
Where is the evidence that supports this belief?

Interpretations

An interpretation is something that you believe to be true about a situation, experience or person. An example might be a colleague who ignores you when arriving at work.

There may be numerous explanations for this behaviour; however, it is not uncommon to be quick to interpret this lack of interaction in a negative way.

Example:

Coachee: They totally ignored me on the way into school, they do not respect me and do not think I'm up to the job!

Coach: What's another way of looking at that
or
Tell me the opposite viewpoint to that?

Assumptions

Past experiences influence how we see the world going forward. We assume that if something has happened a certain way in the past it will happen again in the same way going forward. If the way we are seeing the world is not serving us well then we can challenge our beliefs about how we experience life moving forward.

Example:

Coachee: I am dreading taking my subject test today, it went so badly last time.

Coach: Just because that happened previously, what makes you think it will happen again?

Gremlins

Your 'gremlin' or 'inner critic' can tell yourself you are not good enough in whatever way, shape or form. Gremlins are often the most powerful blocks, core feelings and insecurities that have potentially been embedded for long periods of time. I frequently come across such blocks when coaching leaders in education – they believe they are 'not good enough' or 'do not deserve' to be in the position they have attained. This is frequently described as 'impostor syndrome'. I would say a majority of the leaders I coach suffer from this at some point and I include myself in that. I also witness these blocks in teachers as well as students, in fact just about everyone you come across!

The key to breaking through this block is to bring the 'gremlin' out into the open by creating awareness of it. You can't outrun your mind so, more often than not, simply recognising the gremlin and perhaps naming it, lessens its power[24]. A way to work through a 'gremlin' is through the AIR process:

- **A**wareness: bring the gremlin to the surface, acknowledge your feelings
- **I**ntegration: embrace the gremlin as part of you. This is about accepting your feelings and insecurities.

- **R**elease: let go of the gremlin's control over you and work with it. Once you have acceptance you can then release the energy.

Example:

I was working with the Head of an international school. They had been in post for a couple of years and were brought in to improve the school which had received a disappointing inspection. The job required some people to be moved on due to capability issues, thereby breaking up a settled and vocal staff body. It was a turbulent time as you can imagine. Through coaching the Head realised that their gremlin centred on 'not being up to the job'. Using the AIR process, we firstly became aware of thinking such as 'this was a step too far' and 'I'm not good enough to be in this position'. Through our coaching sessions we began to integrate these feelings into our work. It was perfectly understandable to feel this way as they were taking on a big job (lots of acknowledging); we all have our insecurities, it's OK to have these feelings.

When these feelings came up the Head named them 'Barnaby', telling themselves, here comes Barnaby again! They were then able to begin to accept and release the energy of their gremlin, it wasn't defining them. It was also helpful to look for evidence that they were doing a good job, reframing and getting clarity on situations from a neutral standpoint, not one skewed by negative bias.

Summary of Fundamental coaching skills

A useful first step in evolving your coaching is the utilisation of the Fundamental skills and coaching through the energy blocks. This alone can be hugely powerful across a range of school contexts and settings. If you are new to coaching, it would be wise to spend a few months getting to grips with the Fundamental skills before moving on to more specific application.

It may be that you simply want to incorporate coaching skills into your professional practice but take it no further which is fine. I encourage you to embrace these skills – they can bring huge results.

Application of Fundamental Coaching Skills

In my view, Fundamental coaching skills should be learnt and practised before transitioning to a models-based coaching approach. Models can form the basis of fundamental application and build on the coaching skills outlined previously. It is a mistake for educational coach training to neglect coaching skills and begin a coaching journey by jumping straight into using models, without the understanding and awareness of the skills that underpin a coaching approach. The first, and often forgotten, step in a more formalised coaching approach lies with contracting.

Contracting

Contracting lays the foundation for coaching application; it is the establishment of expectations between coach and coachee. It can be utilised working in formal or informal contexts whether mentoring with trainee teachers or executive coaching with education leaders.

This key coaching process is often missing in education, which is strange given that educators are frequently taught about the importance of establishing expectations for the students and classes that they teach. Contracting can cover the following:

Logistics

- duration of sessions
- timing and frequency
- cancellations
- potential fees
- contact between sessions
- venue

Boundaries

- confidentially
- roles
- responsibilities

- expectations
- conflicts of interest

Ways of working

- face to face
- phone or virtual
- coaching methods
- outcomes
- measurements of success
- preparation or work between sessions[25]

So many issues can arise in coaching partnerships that could have been prevented by simply spending time contracting at the beginning of the process itself.

You don't want to hear things like, 'oh I didn't know that', or 'you never told me that'.

Contracting also has parallels with teachers setting behaviour expectations for the classes they teach (which is explored in Part 2).

Take the time to contract before you commence coaching and revisit if necessary throughout the coaching itself.

Coaching models

Once robust contracting is in place and your Fundamental coaching skills are honed you can progress to embedding them within a structured, solution-focused approach to coaching: a coaching model.

There are multiple coaching models to choose from and they are beneficial in that they are generally easy to remember.

Irrespective of which coaching model you choose to use, successful coaching depends upon incorporating all of the learnt coaching skills throughout the process.

A model on its own is simply a model. I have outlined six well-known coaching models here which can help frame your coaching.

TO GROW

The GROW method coined by John Whitmore[26] in his popular book *Coaching for Performance* is perhaps the most well-known coaching model. Although nearly 40 years old, this model remains a staple in coaching training and in education worldwide.

The addition of 'TO' adds a variation that helps to distinguish the objective for the session itself from short- and longer-term goals. This is a good model to use for performance development and appraisals.

Topic: What do you want to talk about today?

Objective: What would you like to take away from this conversation/session?

Goal (for the short and long term): What are you wanting to achieve?

Reality (checking to explore the current situation): What is currently going on?

Options (including alternative strategies or courses of action): What are your options here?

What is to be done, when and by whom: What will you do?

CLEAR

The CLEAR model, conceived by Peter Hawkins[27] in the early 1980s, pre-dates 'GROW' but in many ways encapsulates a wider coaching approach, with the inclusion of contracting and review to inform development.

I have used this model to run team meetings which is outlined in a coaching way of leading in Part 3. Note the explicit 'listening' stage, which aligns with a focus on a Fundamental coaching skill.

Contracting: Opening the discussion, setting the scope, establishing the desired outcomes, and agreeing the ground rules.

Listening: Using listening the coach helps the coachee develop their understanding of the situation and generate personal insight.

Exploring 1: Helping the coachee to understand the personal impact the situation is having on themselves.

Exploring 2: Challenging the coachee to think through possibilities for future action in resolving the situation.

Action: Supporting the coachee in choosing a way ahead and deciding the next step.

Review: Closing the session, reinforcing ground covered, decisions made and value added. The coach also encourages feedback from the coachee on what was helpful about the process, what was difficult and what they would like to be different in future coaching sessions.

OSKAR

This is another example of an easy-to-follow coaching model, originally established by Karen Whittleworth and Andrew Gilbert in 2002.

This model can be used as part of the instructional coaching process outlined later based around lesson feedback. Note the importance of scaling questioning, as outlined in the Fundamental domain.

Outcome: What would you like to achieve in this session?

Scaling: On a scale of 1 to 10, with 10 representing a wonderful future, and 0 the worst, where are you on that scale?

Know-how and resources: What supports you performing at that number on the scale? How do you do it?

Affirm and action: What is going well? What is the next step?

Review: What is better? How did you make the change? (Note: this step works well at the beginning of the following session)[28]

BASIC

Andy Buck[29] has developed a model which focuses on BASIC steps (Background, Aim, Strategy, Implementation and Commitment). These steps are framed around the qualities, habits and feedback of an effective coaching approach.

I like the question-first approach with this model, as this allows you to understand the context and hold someone's agenda before moving forward.

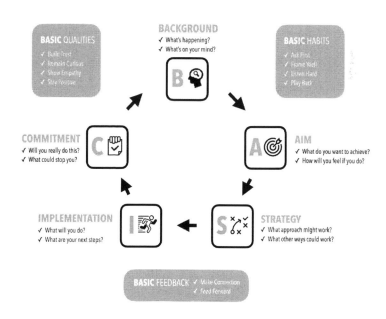

POSITIVE

The POSITIVE model[30] is very much focussed on the 'powerful coaching question' to develop clarity of thought and intention for the coachee. I particularly appreciate the 'Value' stage which supports vision and the motivation towards a goal aligned with the courageous target setting outlined earlier.

Purpose – what is it you want to achieve?

Observations – what have you tried so far?

Strategy – what does success look like for you?

Insight – how committed are you in achieving this goal on a scale of 1 – 10?

Team – who will you share your goal with?

Initiate – when will you start to act on this?

Value – how will you celebrate your success?

Encourage – how are you going with your goals?

Teacher development models

When leading departments and schools I always enjoyed staff development, it was the highlight of the job for me. This is all about getting a balance between development and evaluation. The problems arising from too much emphasis on evaluation for accountability may lead to weak and even hostile relationships between staff and their appraisers with frank discussion about weaknesses unlikely to occur. On the other hand, problems can arise from the emphasis being too much on the individual: professional development may be weaker, teachers are insufficiently challenged, and training and development needs are not guaranteed to be available[31].

The relationship between coaching and performance management structures and procedures is then an interesting one. Many schools are still grappling with the core tension of the relationship between performance management and coaching. Good practice allows coaching to be a performance management tool, not a slave to performance management[32].

A typical school performance management cycle would look something like the below[33] based around three reviews (lesson observations).

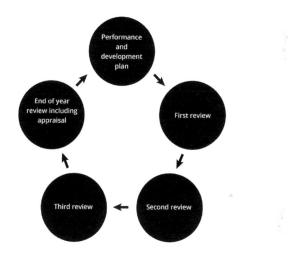

There may well be some peer observations thrown in and potentially some informal opportunities to speak to your line manager, but this is a good illustration of traditional practice in education (in which I also include Higher Education). In the same way that I don't place high value on one-day training sessions as they do not facilitate sustainable development, I also believe the traditional review process above does not have teacher development at its heart.

However, there continues to be exciting developments across the education sector, with a Fundamental coaching approach taking a key role: walkthroughs, unseen observations, instructional coaching and incremental coaching are outlined below.

Walkthroughs

School walkthroughs are implemented in various ways and unlike a classroom observation, which provides a view of a single classroom, a walkthrough creates a school wide picture made up of many small snapshots[34]. The structure also allows an individual to be in a classroom for a short period of time and gain as much information that may be used later to facilitate teachers' reflections about their decisions[35]. The key here is to actually have the time to feedback to teachers during which robust discussions can take place around ways to improve, where you can use your coaching evolution to develop staff.

Teachers want feedback, especially if you are in their classes. This was drilled into me during school inspection training, where generally an inspector is only in lessons for around 20 minutes with restricted time to provide feedback. There is not the time for scrolls of written feedback so sharp and informative observations are needed, such as:

Example:

- Students were engaged in their learning because the class activities were well planned.

Or

- Your targeted questioning was effective because it allowed students to more fully understand key themes.

When providing feedback think about holding a teacher's agenda, engaging higher levels of listening and questioning as previously outlined.

Unseen observations

In unseen observations all the important features of observations take place; planning, discussing, reviewing and back to planning, but without there being an observer present. The emphasis is placed on the teacher's experience of the lesson, predicted through the lesson plan and reflected upon after the lesson itself. It is the teacher's perception of the taught lesson that provokes the basis for the supervisor's work in their interaction with the teacher[36]. The focus is on the dialogue about practice, and this is a critical vehicle for professional learning[37]. This is very much aligned to the approaches in the Transformative coaching domain (see Chapter 3) which will help support you with opportunities to promote fruitful and meaningful dialogue throughout the entire process.

Unseen observations can work in the following way:

- Teacher identifies focus lesson
- Teacher prepares and sends supervisor/observer a copy of the draft lesson plan to comment on
- Teacher and supervisor discuss lesson
- Teacher produces final draft of the lesson
- Teacher writes up reflective account of the lesson
- Teacher and supervisor meet for professional dialogue to discuss lesson
- Teacher writes up a series of forwarding actions

Being trained in the Fundamental domain can really benefit supervisors frame reflections with teachers, developing their professional conversations throughout the above process.

Brookfield's "lenses" model[38] is widely used as a reflective tool in Initial Teacher Training courses and can be incorporated at the 'meeting for professional dialogue' stage above. This advocates appreciation of different viewpoints within a given situation. Essentially the main stakeholders in a lesson observation context are:

- teacher (autobiographical)
- students
- colleagues
- perspective(s) derived from theoretical literature

Consideration of alternative viewpoints is one of the hallmarks of deep reflection and in alignment with the Systemic coaching domain (see Chapter 2). Unseen observations can be an effective way of teacher development, however, there has been concern that this approach may not be suitable for teachers who need more input and support. Perhaps you could adapt your lesson observations depending on the teacher, or have a suite of lesson observations from formal to unseen.

Instructional coaching

Another popular example of models-based coaching is Jim Knight's Instructional Coaching model[39] based around the setting of goals and providing support for teachers. There appears to be some confusion around instructional coaching, with differing interpretations of the approach and I would invite you to research this area in depth before using in your setting.

Rather than a one formal observation or a brief visit as part of a walkthrough, in instructional coaching the coach will engage with the teacher on a sustained basis over time, seeing them teach regularly and meeting to discuss their progress regularly.

Each time there is help to identify problems and associated action steps; helping them to sustain practice on specific aspects of their craft. The log of action steps serves to inform the process as it moves through various cycles of review and improvement.'[40]

Instructional coaches partner with teachers to:

- analyse the current reality
- set goals
- identify and explain teaching strategies to meet goals
- provide support until goals are met[41]

This is an approach that is used both in schools and as part of Initial Teacher Training, with strong Fundamental coaching skills such as goal setting and action planning. Firstly, instructional coaches position teachers as partners, as you would find in a typical coaching set up rather than a top-down expert and novice hierarchy.

This engenders the trust and respect associated with being a professional educator, in line with the unseen observation approach.

Secondly, an instructional coach will use what is known as the **Impact Cycle** to frame the process, which is made up of three stages:

- identify
- learn
- improve

Identify

In the identify stage the focus is on understanding the **current reality** and **goal setting** in order to teach strategically.

Understanding the **current reality** can be done through videoing or observing live lessons, learning from students and reviewing observation data. Ideally you would get feedback from all three, but do what is possible.

The videoing of lessons remains a bone of contention across education, although the recent pandemic has made this the 'norm' in some lesson contexts. Whilst there are some real benefits, teachers can also become anxious and a little wary as to where and how recordings will be used. I have found that even in its simplest form, witnessing your own teaching can have a powerful effect regardless of any further coaching support.

I remember noticing how many times I said 'fantastic' to the students in my lessons and the pace at which I progressed lessons was a real eye-opener! Essentially, in the same way diagnostic assessments are used in leadership, this is an excellent way to see the current reality, although this shouldn't be a labelling of practice, rather a snapshot of practice.

In terms of learning from students, small focus groups can provide a safe space from which to glean information. Once again you can leverage your Fundamental coaching skills such as active listening, acknowledging, summarising and questioning to illicit responses in an informal way. Think back to the idea of holding a space in your coaching evolution.

The goal here is not to influence answers, so be neutral and non-directive when coaching, leave space for students to answer and do not lead students down a specific path. You can also use student work to help support the process which can provide prompts for the students themselves. In relation to an observation, mirror the approach taken in the unseen observation process in which there is a meeting before the lesson where the planning and strategies can be discussed.

The next focus of the identify stage is to **set goals** based on the current reality findings: identify what is happening and forward the action. You could even use the AIM SMART model for goal setting as outlined previously. As ever, utilise your Fundamental coaching skills to get robust and achievable goals in place. Once you have agreed goals with your teaching partner it is important to set a schedule of further coaching sessions to better understand how to move forward.

Learn

In the learn stage, the instructional coach in a sense turns back from a neutral non-directive to directive approach. This supports the coach as an engaged actor (as outlined in the Transformative coaching domain in Chapter 3). It is important for the instructional coach to have a strong teaching repertoire to call upon. Once the teacher's goals have been set, the instructional coach now creates a checklist for each goal, or as Jim Knight[42] refers to it, a playbook.

The playbook outlines how the teacher can develop their goals. For example, if one of the goals is about behaviour management then a goal could be to effectively transition the class into the room.

The checklist for this could be: greet each student at the door, have a set and understood seating plan for the class and have a task on the board ready to engage the students.

The instructional coach would then model this approach and invite the teacher to observe their lesson. Another way could be to team teach the start of a lesson together or to rehearse the process without any students present. The key point is the opportunity for the teacher to witness and understand the strategies, in order to better enact and achieve them.

Improve

The final stage in instructional coaching is about ensuring that the teacher is progressing towards their goals – as such there needs to be some degree of flexibility. In coaching sessions, you can once again utilise your Fundamental coaching skills to understand progress made and potential issues.

This will involve the instructional coach reviewing evidence (as per the current reality stage) to see if targets are being met and if not, what needs to change. There is accountability with the instructional coach supporting the teacher to get things done.

Further coaching sessions can then be focussed around action plans against set goals or indeed the formulation of other goals that come to light.

Instructional coaching has the power to support teachers to manage the complexity of their classroom, no matter what their phase or subject[43]. To implement instructional coaching in schools there needs to be a big drive to upskill teachers in the Fundamental coaching domain and the Impact Cycle; time is required for such upskilling, a scarce resource in schools.

Incremental coaching

Incremental coaching has a similar approach to instructional coaching in that it is a regular, frequent and ongoing cycle of short observations and action-based follow-up conversations to help teachers develop specific aspects of practice.

One-to-one incremental coaching is tailored to each teacher's needs. Example topics include timing lessons better, ending lessons calmly and techniques to engage all pupils in class discussions[44]. The cycle (see diagram overleaf) is based around a coaching-style relationship with the teacher again framed around goal setting, modelling and practice to embed.

In terms of impact, a study commissioned by Ambition School Leadership[45] found that most coachees (82%) strongly agreed their practice had benefitted their teaching and 75% strongly agreed that incremental coaching had helped school improvement. This is further proof that coaching offers an effective, personalised approach to teacher development.

Coaching is a form of collaborative CPD and can be a strong dimension of teachers' professional learning in school. There also needs to be time for coaching to be built into the school timetable and directed time and appropriate finance to fund this if coaching is to thrive[46].

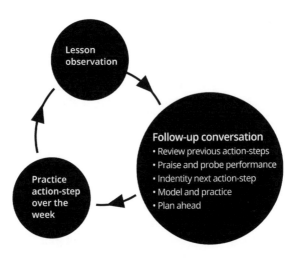

When to use a Fundamental coaching approach?

Skills and models are a good place to start with coaching. The reliance on an easy-to-follow and simple framework to implement coaching in schools, where time is limited, is appealing. Schools all over the world engage with this approach for:

- whole staff training in the Fundamental coaching approach to begin to develop a coaching culture
- one-to-one appraisals and performance management
- teacher development
- peer support for all staff and students
- student leaders' development

A note of caution on the use of coaching as an intervention strategy for underachieving staff: whilst there is merit in utilising coaching skills, you need to be clear if coaching is indeed the correct medium of engagement. In some circumstances it may be more appropriate to adopt a more directive, mentoring approach in relation to capability.

Limitations of the Fundamental domain

This domain is the most common in use across the education sector and certainly has a place. You may notice a common theme weaving through the models I have included. There is a predominance of goals, identifying problems and solutions, and moving forward. Education can be obsessed with solution-focussed coaching, to the detriment of the coaching impact. In isolation a solution-focussed approach is unlikely to prove useful when considering the complexity of settings and functions in a school[47].

There is also an issue with potentially shoe-horning conversations into a model simply because the coach is focussed on following it. Coaching using a purely models-based approach can be linear and reductionist[48]. As author of the GROW model himself, John Whitmore, states: 'If you think about it, a model doesn't say anything about coaching itself'[49].

Focussing purely on solutions can also leave people feeling inadequate if they do not meet targets, and potentially overwhelmed when faced with trying to meet goals, leading to stress. Following a pre-prescribed model can leave little room for truly transformative dialogue and is – in my opinion – often misused as a performance management tool for underachieving staff.

Summary

- One-to-one coaching relationship
- Skills and models based
- Input and output process
- Onus on the coach to master the basic seven coaching skills
- Framed around a non-directive coaching approach
- The focus is on goal setting and finding solutions to problems

References

1. Van Nieuwerburgh, C. (2012) Coaching in Education, Karnac, London, UK
2. Lawrence, P. & Moore, A. (2019) Coaching in Three Dimensions, Routledge, UK
3. Thomson, B. (2013) Non-directive Coaching, Critical Publishing Ltd, Cheshire, UK
4. iPEC (2013), Coaching Training Manual, US
5. Van Nieuwerburgh, C., (2017) An Introduction to Coaching Skills, A Practical Guide, Sage, London
6. Lawrence, P., Hill, S., Priestland, A., Forrestal, C., Rommerts, F., Hyslop, I. & Manning, M. (2019) The Tao of Dialogue, Routledge Focus, UK
7. Van Nieuwerburgh, C. (2017) An Introduction to Coaching Skills, A Practical Guide, Sage, London
8. Vogt, E., Brown, J. & Isaacs, D. (2003) The Art of Powerful Questions, Whole Systems Associates, US
9. Whitmore, J. (1992) Coaching for Performance, Nicholas Brealey Publishing, London, UK
10. Bungay Stanier, M. (2016) The Coaching Habit, Box of Crayons Press, US
11. Van Nieuwerburgh, C. (2017) An Introduction to Coaching Skills, A Practical Guide, Sage, London
12. Locke & Latham (2002) in Jones, R. (2021) Coaching with Research in Mind, Routledge, UK
13. Price, R. (2021) The Coach's Handbook, Routledge, UK
14. Lawrence, P. (2019) The Systemic Coach White Paper, part 1 of 4, Centre for Coaching in Organisations, Australia
15. iPEC (2013) Coaching Training Manual, US
16. Day, I. (2012) The 'Olympic' Approach to Setting and Achieving Courageous Goals, the Bulletin of the Association for Coaching, July 2012, Issue 9
17& 18. Prywes, Y. and Mah, E. (2019) Seeing Polaris: A Call to Integrate Visual Images into Coaching Action Plans, Philosophy of Coaching: An International Journal Vol.4, No.1, May 2019
19. Strozzi-Heckler, R. (2014) The Art of Somatic Coaching, North Atlantic Books, US
20 & 21. Quest, P. (2002) Reiki for Life, Piatkus, UK
22. Schneider, B. (2008) Energy Leadership, John Wiley and Sons, US
23 & 24. iPEC (2013) Coaching Training Manual, US
25. Morgan, K. (2019) The Coach's Survival Guide, McGraw Hill, London
26. Whitmore, J. (1992) Coaching for Performance, Nicholas Brealey Publishing, London, UK
27. Hawkins, P. (2012) Creating a coaching culture, McGraw Hill, UK
28. Thomson, B. (2013) Non-directive Coaching, Critical Publishing Ltd, Cheshire, UK
29. Buck, A. (2020) The BASIC Coaching Method, Cadogan Press, UK

30. Libri, V. (2004) Beyond GROW: In Search of Acronyms and Coaching Models, The International Journal of Mentoring and Coaching in Coaching Models in Education, A Think Piece Working Paper by Ruth Whiteside in Working Papers, CollectivED - The Centre for Mentoring, Coaching and Professional Learning (July 2020)

31. Middlewood, D. in Bush & Bell (2002) The Principles and Practice of Educational Management, Sage, London

32. Lofthouse, R., Leat, D. & Towler, C. (2010) Coaching For Teaching and Learning: A Practical Guide For Schools, CfBT Education Trust, UK

33. Gold, J. & Bratton, J. (2007) Human Resource Management, Palgrave MacMillan, UK

34. Richardson, J. (2001) Seeing Through New Eyes, National Staff Development Council, Tools for Schools, US

35. Downey, J., Steffy, B., English, F., Frase, L. & Poston Jr, W. (2004) Changing School Supervisory Practice One Teacher at a Time, Corwin Press, US

36. O'Leary, M. (2014 & 2020) Classroom Observation, Routledge, London

37. Danielson, C. (2009) Talk about Teaching: Leading Professional Conversations, Corwin Press, US

38. Brookfield, S. (1995) Becoming a Critically Reflective Teacher. 1st ed. San Francisco: Jossey-Bass

39. Knight, J. (2018) The Impact Cycle, Corwin Press, US

40. Sherrington, T. (2021) Time To Replace 'Formal Observation' Systems With Instructional Coaching for Everyone, (https://teacherhead.com/2021/01/28/time-to-replace-formal-observation-systems-with-instructional-coaching-for-everyone-cpd/)

41 & 42. Knight, J. (2018) The Impact Cycle, Corwin Press, US

43. Fardon, S. (2021) Balancing The Purposes of Instructional Coaching, (www.ambition.org.uk/blog/balancing-purposes-instructional-coaching/)

44 & 45. Ambition School Leadership (2017) Incremental Coaching: How Can It Help Your Teachers Develop?, UK

46. Lofthouse, R., Leat, D. & Towler, C. (2010) Coaching For Teaching and Learning: A Practical Guide For Schools, CfBT Education Trust, UK

47. Lawrence, P. (2019) The Systemic Coach White Paper, Centre for Coaching in Organisations, Australia

48. Cavanagh, S. (2013) in Wright, A., McLean Walsh, M. & Tennyson, S. (2019) Systemic Coaching Supervision: Responding to the Complex Challenges of Our Time, Philosophy of Coaching: An International Journal, Vol.4, No.1, May 2019

49. Wildflower, L. (2013) The Hidden History of Coaching, McGraw Hill, US

The Systemic Domain

Systemic coaching definition:

Systemic coaching recognises that learning and development happens not inside the individual but in dynamic engagement with the wider systems they are part of and relate with; it reflects that we are part of communities and cultures that shape our language, ways of being, thinking and doing[1].

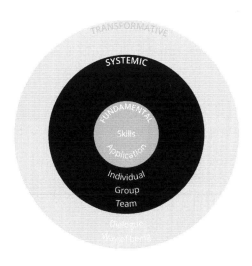

Building upon the coaching skills and application outlined in the Fundamental domain the Systemic domain is the next step in your coaching evolution (see diagram showing the three domains and their subdomains, above). Recent discussion around systemic approaches to coaching have more emphasis on the context people operate in[2].

The Systemic domain acknowledges that educational contexts are dynamic and unpredictable, stuff is always happening, and people are forever attempting to make sense of change through conversations with each other[3]. This is about having a broader perspective, looking beyond the individual to the patterns and dynamics at play in your environment.

Each person's system is made up of different parts, such as family, profession, community, and social context[4]. When coaching in the Systemic domain, you need to look at people not in a vacuum but rather acknowledging the backdrop to their lives, in order to inform work. That is not to say you should get caught up in their storyline but merely have an appreciation and awareness of their context.

A fitting analogy from John Whittington[5] talks about a peacock's tail: each eyespot in the tail represents one system in your life. This really opens up your field of vision and talks of the deep patterns, hidden loyalties, and experiences of belonging in each system you have passed through and how they inform your way of being in the world.

With this in mind, it is wise to acknowledge your own personal experiences outside of your professional life when coaching – these are always integrated in some way shape or form in wider systemic work. In the same way, as a teacher we need to be mindful of the attitude and approach we bring to lessons and as a coach we must reflect on what values *we* are bringing to the coaching table and not to let these influence our coaching work.

The Systemic domain also requires you to be more reflective and self-aware than in Fundamental ways of coaching. For educationalists there is a variety of stakeholders involved (see diagram opposite).

These stakeholders can be a gateway to the systems at play and allow us to better understand how to coach effectively.

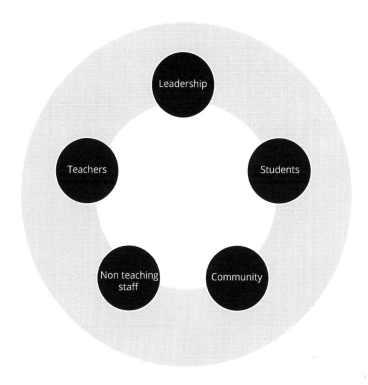

In terms of leadership, stakeholders involved will include senior and middle leaders as well as your board of governors and potentially school proprietors. Community can cover parents as well as further community links with businesses and local council or government organisations for example.

Non-teaching staff, teachers and students are self-explanatory. With an increased understanding of the stakeholders involved, your coaching development can progress. The Systemic domain is split into three sub domains:

- Individual
- Group
- Team

Individual Systemic Coaching

Individual systemic definition:

Individual systemic coaching is a collaborative and dialogical inquiry between two people, exploring how the client can learn and develop in relation to the worlds they are embedded within, in a way that creates positive benefit for them and all the nested systems of which they are part[6].

It could be argued that in one-to-one coaching we are always taking into account a variety of systems, as illustrated in some of the models outlined in the Fundamental domain. However, having a 'systemic mindset' is key (outlined in more depth in Part 3, a coaching way of leading).

For example, when I am coaching school leaders the focus may be on the challenges posed from colleagues, school governing body, students and community as well as their personal context.

This may also necessitate interviewing people around the person I am working with to understand context. When sessions are initially focussed on professional aspects this may also bleed into the personal.

I find system mapping provides a clear, visual way of developing an awareness of how someone operates in relation with others. It can be an extremely informative process that allows the coachee to gain more clarity on their current situation within a one-to-one session.

This is about helping the coachee to recognise and see themselves within the system to which they belong, as well as being aware of the narratives and stories that are present.

My work with education leaders usually follows a mapping process – it can last for an hour or more, or form a shorter component of a session. I find that mapping can work well in initial individual coaching sessions when beginning to understand the context and dynamics at play within your coachee's setting.

Mapping can be broken down into three separate stages[7]:

- interview
- mapping
- closure

Interview

This stage is centred on discovering the context to a particular issue or challenge by asking questions. Draw on the Fundamental domain coaching skills and start by getting the coachee to briefly summarise the issue.

For example:

- What's on your mind?

Or

- What is your biggest challenge currently?

Secondly, ascertain what will be different if the issue or challenge is resolved. You are not looking for a goal here, but a feeling or resolution that you can return to throughout the coaching process.

For example:

- If your current challenge is resolved, what would be different?

Lastly, ask about the map itself in terms of key players such as people or elements involved with the issue or challenge. Ideally, begin by identifying four of these elements at the most.

I find that coachees commonly identify line managers or work colleagues, and elements such as the environment in which they work.

Mapping

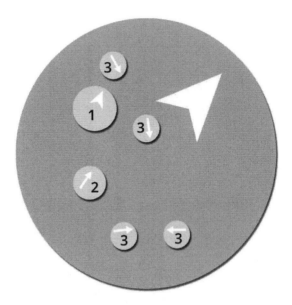

The mapping stage is best demonstrated through the previous diagram[8]: an example of a map of the school system in which a coachee (a CEO in this case) is embedded. The following example shows how the process can work.

Example:

We (coach and coachee) first agreed on what the boundaries of the map were, in this case the circle, representing the school (system). The large white arrow depicts the current trajectory of the school (upwardly mobile). We agreed that the closer each piece was placed to another, the more entwined the relationships, and the greater distance between pieces represented more distant relationships.

The largest circle piece on the board (1) represents the CEO. I asked them to place themselves where they think they sat within the system.

The choice of position near the top of the school hierarchy, with their arrow pointing upwards in parallel to the white arrow, symbolised their alignment to the overall school vision.

Next, the coachee placed a school principal (2) below them to symbolise their current position within the team. The coachee was keen to point out that this was not a hierarchy, more a representation of current thinking and roles between them. The principal was not that experienced in role but was keen to develop and grow as depicted by their upward facing arrow.

Four whole-school deputy heads (3) were identified in the interview stage. These were placed in the circle, with the distance between the coachee and others depicting the range of current relationships.

Two deputies at the bottom of the map had a fractious relationship as illustrated by their proximity and arrows facing each other. The coachee also placed them at the bottom of the circle due to their current attitude towards school improvement, which the coachee felt was resistant.

The other two deputies were placed near the coachee, symbolising their willingness to act on feedback. The coachee also saw more of them around school. The two downward arrows related to a feeling that they still needed support however.

If my coachee were to be absent, for example, the coachee was not confident that the deputies would keep up the standard of performance.

As coach, I framed and facilitated the session by asking questions to clarify and prompt the coachee's thinking but they themselves placed and mapped the context accordingly. This can be done virtually or face to face. Your role as coach is to stand back and be non-directive, as per the Fundamental domain.

You want your coachee to explain their current thinking about the system in this visual format, including where people (players) sit within this and how relationships are viewed.

Closure

By progressing through the mapping exercise, this allows your coachee the opportunity to come out of their situation, gain clarity and see things from a different perspective. In the closure stage, you need to ask what new insights and thoughts your coachee has in relation to their current situation.

This stage allows your coachee to become free to see new possibilities. In the specific example given above, my coachee decided that they needed to intervene with the two deputy heads (3) and so begin to reconcile relationships. This included meeting them more consistently to develop a sound working relationship. A personal development plan was out in place for the school principal (2) for upskilling around how to effectively run a school. The two deputies near the top were invited to lead whole-school training to involve these two individuals more in school development.

With the mapping in place, you can continue with the session or simply close.

Tip:

A note here in terms of goal setting: when beginning to map with a coachee I find it beneficial to progress the map session by session rather than set the system up to reflect the coachee's desired end point.

You want to start as things are, allowing your coachee to understand that small increments in an ever-shifting system can be very impactful. Change comes incrementally.

Group Coaching

Group coaching definition:

Group coaching is the coaching of individuals with a group context, where the group members take turns to be the focal point while the other group members become part of the coaching resource for that individual. The group of people may then have a shared interest but no collective responsibility to deliver results[9].

Once you are up to speed with Fundamental coaching skills and processes, alongside an awareness of the systems in which *you* belong, you can now play an active part in the development of others through facilitation of professional dialogue and reflection. The planning and delivery of professional group coaching widens the value of coaching beyond the individual, building skills across your colleagues and setting.

Action learning

Action learning is an educational process where people work and learn together by tackling real issues and through reflection. When action learning is undertaken in conjunction with others, e.g., in a small group, the group is referred to as an action learning set[10]. Action learning sets provide a framework similar to group coaching.

They are simple to use and utilise Fundamental domain skills such as contracting, powerful questioning and active listening to enable the coach to prompt group members to tackle their challenges.

The use of trios in professional development is common in education settings, particularly for teacher development.

Traditionally this consists of three teachers working together across a period of time, sharing good practice. Action learning develops this approach by expecting group members to actually coach each other. It is here that we see the importance of understanding fundamental coaching skills at an individual level in order to impact wider institutional growth.

Action learning set

An action learning set can be flexible in approach but generally is made up of peers who work at similar levels within a school or organisation, with some core elements that draw heavily on Fundamental coaching:

- Group size of (approximately) six people
- Action on real tasks or issues at work, with learning from reflections on actions taken
- Tasks or issues are individual rather than collective and chosen by the individual
- Questioning is used as the main coaching tool to help people to proceed with their tasks
- Group coach facilitates sessions
- A contract to meet regularly
- An open approach to issues
- Reflection at a pace that allows time to think[11]

Action learning has the advantage of rotating different roles, such as leader, within the set. In a group of six people, each leader gets time to think about their own issue, with coaching from their peers; they then provide that coaching to the other participants in the group when it is their thinking time.

As the group coach (facilitator) your role is to help them to stick to coaching, rather than stray into giving advice. Despite appearing helpful, advice is not as effective as using a coaching approach to develop independent, critical thinking[12].

You are looking to develop enquiry in a safe space so with support from the coach, group members choose a goal and then learn from each stage of the learning cycle.

See the action learning set diagram opposite which illustrates the process.

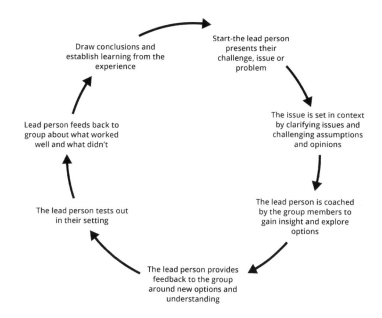

Holding a group

I briefly outlined the importance of 'holding' in the Fundamental domain as part of the key coaching skills, but this will now need to be developed further when working with more than one person.

Effective coaches have the capacity to hold their coachees; effective group coaches must have something more. They must have the ability to hold a group of coachees simultaneously, containing more difficult feelings and stranger projections than with one person[13].

This is where I see teachers and educators in general having a head start in some respects. For example, being able to deal with a class full of students lends itself to the idea of managing and facilitating a number of different people at once. We are also used to delivering meetings and training in our schools.

How can group coaching work in practice?

Group coaching can be an excellent way of creating synergy and developing shared learning and understanding across a range of settings, and indeed the education sector as a whole. People within a group do not have to be located in a single work setting. I commonly work with a group of coachees, for example headteachers, from different schools, regions and countries over the course of a day, with each coachee having an hour to explore their challenges as outlined in the process above. Example topics can include how to effectively communicate or how to run successful meetings. It is a superb platform to share best practice and learn from other schools and peers.

Keeping time at the end of each learning set, to reflect on the process as a group and to enhance practice, is important in the same way you would review a session in a one-to-one coaching conversation.

You can be as flexible as time allows; if time is short I sometimes spread the sessions out over a longer period of time, six weeks for example, to allow one set to take place each week. Alternatively, it is possible to conduct this over the course of a day with all members of the group ready with action points to try out in their setting. I then revisit the group at a later date to ascertain the effectiveness of the actions. This stage can also be facilitated by the group without the coach present if needed.

An example of how this works with a group in one specific setting (ie., the same work location) is group coaching middle leaders through appraisal feedback challenges, teaching processes or behaviour management techniques. It is possible to combine different departmental and phase heads from across your school in groups.

You facilitate sessions in line with the action learning set (as per the diagram above) with each person taking it in turn to share challenges, questions or scenarios. In each subsequent round (or set), coaching skills improve and there becomes a greater sense of shared meaning and understanding, developing a more cohesive group whilst also benefitting the individual.

Group coaching can also be an effective way of developing a whole staff body on a training day, in targeted groups such as middle leaders or departments, and students themselves. You can also engage the wider school community through such a strategy. For example, a parent committee coaching each other on how to support their children's home working, or a group of students coaching each other on the best way to learn in classes. The key to help facilitate the best thinking through shared experiences.

I have found that, due to the very nature of our profession, teachers are well placed to deliver this professional learning. Ideally, if the members of the groups also have an understanding of Fundamental coaching skills, that will assist in the initial group work and development of coaching conversations.

The success of a group coaching approach can be judged by the continuation of the action learning over time *without* facilitator involvement in a self-sustaining way.

Tip:

It can be common for the group to not listen properly to the lead person or perhaps jump in too early with advice. If this happens set a timer for two minutes with an instruction that no one is allowed to talk except for the lead person. This gives space for the group to listen and understand the challenge. After the initial two minutes the group is allowed to ask open-ended questions for a further two to five minutes. After this, group conversation can open up more fully.

Team Coaching

Team coaching definition:

Unlike group coaching, team coaching is the coaching of a whole team that has a collective purpose and objective which all members are jointly responsible for fulfilling[14].

What is a team?

A team can be described as a collection of talented individuals: 'a relatively small group of people with complementary skills committed to a common purpose, performance goals and ways of working together for which they hold themselves accountable'[15]. Effective teams can:

- establish performance goals which underpin, support and act as stepping stones to common objectives
- generate work that could not be generated by individual team members
- establish ways of working together that promote and support high levels of cooperation to help the team learn and create new ways of working
- establish high levels of accountability

In the Fundamental domain and in individual systemic coaching your focus is the person in front of you. It is framed around individual development, to overcome problems and enhance performance in your coachee's current role. However, in team coaching the focus is on the team and its relationship with the wider systems of which it is a part. As the coach, you are working with a collective, to promote whole team learning and development. Individuals feed into this but the coaching is focussed around the team itself. The aim is to improve the team and bring greater value, not focus on the individuals within it, although this should be a by-product of the work.

Team coaching helps teams work together, with others and within their wider environment, creating lasting change by developing safe and trusting relationships, better ways of working and new thinking, so that they maximise their collective potential, purpose and performance goals[16]. Team coaching is a real growth area and one in which education and educators can find real benefit. In a team situation, different people are working together and the coach needs to be aware of many more dynamics when compared with individual coaching. This is why it is necessary to have a sound grasp and understanding of the previous coaching domains so as to equip yourself thoroughly.

A word of caution when working with teams if you, as coach, are in fact part of the team. Whilst the coaching work can still be carried out you will need to be aware of the politics, relationship dynamics and bias that you bring. Team coaching and facilitation is best carried out by an external person for maximum benefit, but you will be able to take ideas from my exploration of team coaching and adapt to your setting.

Six lenses of systemic team coaching

According to John Leary-Joyce and Hilary Lines[17], to effectively coach teams you will need to be aware of the following six lenses:

- individual
- inter-personal
- team tasks (objectives and purpose)
- team relationships
- stakeholder interfaces
- wider context

Through an understanding of each of the six lenses you as a coach can begin to understand how they relate to and influence each other when working with a team. I find these lenses a great starting point with which to understand the current situation and ask questions around these themes when first working with a team. This can take a few sessions or form a great first day of a coaching day with your team. The following example is taken from a whole day session coaching a team of teachers from a secondary school department in an international school in Bangkok, Thailand.

This took place in a shared space outside of the school environment.

Example:

Individual
We explored individual teacher perspectives and issues in terms of job description such as pedagogy, marking, reports and responsibilities. It was clear that there was general consensus on these but it was a sound starting point to reiterate key understanding. I found that the more experienced staff were quick to explain items here – as a coach be sure

to invite feedback from all parties. It was also clear that the current description of their jobs was not up to date, an issue that was fed back to senior management.

Interpersonal

We then discussed working with their immediate departmental colleagues and wider school departments. We explored the dynamics and how these impacted the team as a whole. I was quite direct in challenging the team to reflect upon the potential hierarchy within the department based on longevity of service (years spent in the school). It was clear the department was close knit but had strong views on how their team was perceived across the school. They felt undervalued in comparison to other departments.

Team tasks

The next stage was identifying specific teaching responsibilities and collaborative tasks such as extra-curricular work. We discussed how the department was operating currently and what the team needed to develop collectively. There was scope to further explore team focus and strategy, linking to their departmental development plan.

Team relationships

We then reflected on how teachers in the team collaborate and work together day to day. Individuals took it in turns to put forward ideas about how this could be developed.

The priorities centred on enhanced departmental meeting time and revisiting a clear 'standard of performance' in relation to understanding each other from a more personal perspective. Actions included developing a weekly coffee morning where work talk was off limits.

Stakeholder interfaces

We then spent time exploring how the department interacted with different people in their school system, such as parents, leadership, non-teaching staff as well as visiting practitioners. The challenges were discussed, with parents being a particular issue. It was decided that the department would attempt to get in front of this issue by sending a monthly bulletin out to parents with frequently asked questions answered.

Wider systemic context
Finally, the conversation centred on education policy, examination and assessment changes. The department asked themselves what they were doing to keep informed. One action was to submit a proposal to the senior team to ask for funding to attend examination training.

As you can see, once you have an idea of the issues as viewed through each of the lenses you can then be flexible in how you coach and approach situations. It may be that you begin by gaining an understanding of individual perspectives before widening your reach; alternatively, you might begin with the wider systemic context. The key here is to have an awareness of each lens and work within them and between them accordingly to provide value to the team you are working with.

Tip:

If you are leading a team in your setting, use the above six lenses as part of your team meetings. You could structure a series of meeting agendas around lenses to ensure that your team is continually reflecting and developing within the changing environment it is part of. For example, you could start with 'team tasks' and discuss how your team needs to develop collaboration across its day-to-day work.

Team coaching stages

The 'creating the team edge' coaching model[18] provides us with a useful template for a team coaching programme which I have adapted below. There are four core stages to team coaching with the additional flexibility to run workshops and training depending on team needs in between these core elements.

Stage 1: Contracting and discovery

Carry out initial contracting with the team (see section in Chapter 1 on contracting) including the reasons for coaching and team need. Aim to get buy in around team purpose and how things will be run.

Drawing on the Fundamental domain skills I suggest using these five questions to prompt understanding of team need:

i) What can only this team uniquely do together that it could not do apart? This helps the team discover their purpose and responsibilities.

ii) How does this team want to be known or described? This helps to create actions which will craft their identity.

iii) How aware is the team of how it engages with the wider systems and stakeholders it is part of? This provides clarity on current performance and targets.

iv) What does the future require of this team? This focusses longer term thinking.

v) What is the one question this team needs to ask itself? This open up exploration of dialogue e.g., what happens if our new timetable system, despite all the planning, doesn't work smoothly[19]?

Stage 2: Initial coaching

Develop an understanding of the team, its players and context through initial one-to-one coaching and interviews with each team member and relevant people linked to the team. As an external coach coming into work settings I tend to allocate and hour per person per session for this initial coaching. I also aim to have at least two one-to-one sessions before coming back to the team setting. I sometimes use the six lenses of systemic team coaching outlined above as a framework when first undertaking initial individual coaching.

If you are a departmental line manager, appraisal or training time could be utilised for this. You can also incorporate one of the coaching models outlined in the Fundamental domain to help frame conversations.

Stage 3: Co-design coaching

Once you have coached individuals and begun to form relationships, come back to the team to decide next steps. As a coach you can agree to feedback elements of the individual coaching sessions. I tend to provide a general summary, being careful not to name people. This also involves co-creating and designing the proposed development journey and timeline based on the needs of the individuals and team as a whole. It may be that this stage is focussed on delivering training in certain areas.

The following are example topics that I have used as workshop sessions when working with an educational trust in London.

Example:

- *Workshop 1: building relationships both inside and outside the team, developing team identity and purpose*

- *Workshop 2: developing shared understanding on team tasks and ways of working and development planning*

- *Workshop 3: developing coaching as a way of promoting learning across the trust*

Stage 4: Evaluation

Review the process and feedback areas for development. This stage may necessitate further sessions on any areas that may not have been successful at first. When working with the educational trust in London for example, we found that more work was needed on developing coaching across trust schools. This then led to revisiting Stage 2 once again to plan and deliver more coaching training to non-teaching staff.

As you can see there is the scope to design the team coaching programme as the team sees fit. It is also important to understand that you may want to invite others into the workshops to support and deliver sessions.

For example, it may be that you want an external person to support coaching fundamentals or for developing expertise on appraisals. It may be that you prefer a wellbeing expert to deliver a session on healthy working.

Consider utilising your team coaching expertise across appropriate teams in your school or organisation, such as inviting teaching and learning teams, pastoral teams or administrative and operational staff teams to feed into training. Such a co-coaching approach can work well.

In summary, your systemic coaching skills will allow you the flexibility to design a team coaching programme as you see fit for your setting. The crucial (if obvious) thing to remember at every stage is that you are working with a team, rather than focussing on individuals.

When to use a Systemic coaching approach

Here are some suggested contexts:

- Individual coaching with middle and senior leaders
- Coaching in groups and teams across departments, phases and wider school or organisation community
- Helping to support the development of teams across your setting, eg., helping senior teams develop vision, mission, objectives, planning, and training
- Helping to develop shared understanding of education dynamics and key players to drive improvement

Limitations of the systemic domain

There is a danger that if we focus too much on the system itself we lose sight of what we need and stop us from understanding what is in front of us! Whilst there is more engagement with different people and contexts in a systemic coaching approach, the premise is still facilitation and non-directive in nature.

By acting as a neutral coach you are potentially missing out on drawing on your own experiences and perspective. There could be missed opportunities for the coachee(s) to co-create with you if the skills and knowledge of the coach are ignored.

There is no doubt that the onus is on the coach to master more progressive coaching skills and processes in this domain. The presumption remains that systems and hierarchy are in play which, as we have seen, have the potential to limit honest dialogue. There can also be extra expense incurred in involving external facilitators for team coaching.

Ideally, before taking part in team coaching, staff are first skilled in the Fundamental coaching domain, which can take time and resource.

Summary

- Systemic coaching domain contains three sub domains: individual, group and team
- Focusses on developing a wider and broader perspective of setting and dynamics beyond that of the individual
- Awareness of the different stakeholders
- Includes mapping, action learning and team coaching processes such as the six lenses of systemic team coaching

References

1. Hawkins, P. & Turner, E. (2020) System Coaching, Routledge, UK
2. Wright, A., McLean Walsh, M. & Tennyson, S. (2019) Systemic Coaching Supervision: Responding to the Complex Challenges of Our Time, Philosophy of Coaching: An International Journal, Vol.4, No.1 May 2019
3. Lawrence, P., The Systemic Coach, White Paper, The Centre for Coaching in Organisations, October 2019
4. Widdowson & Barbour (2021) in Passmore, P. (2021) The Coaches' Handbook, Routledge, UK
5. Whittington, J. (2020) System Coaching and Constellations, KoganPage, UK
6. Hawkins, P. & Turner, E. (2020), System Coaching, Routledge, UK
7. Whittington, J. (2020) System Coaching and Constellations, KoganPage, UK
8. Diagram adapted from Whittington, J. (2020) System Coaching and Constellations, KoganPage, UK
9. Hawkins, P. & Turner, E. (2020) System Coaching, Routledge, UK
10. Walia, S. & Marks-Maran, D. (2014) Leadership Development Through Action Learning Sets: An Evaluation Study, Nurse Education in Practice (doi: 10.1016/j.nepr.2014.06.004.)
11. Thornton, C. (2016) Group and Team Coaching, Routledge, London
12. Norma, C. (2019) (https://trustedcoachdirectory.com/how-action-learning-sets-can-support-a-culture-of-coaching-in-organisations/)
13. Thornton, C. (2016) Group and Team Coaching, Routledge, London
14. Hawkins, P. & Turner, E. (2020) System Coaching, Routledge, UK
15. Whitaker, D. (1999) The Spirit of Teams, The Crowood Press Ltd, UK
16. Widdowson and Barbour (2019) in Passmore, P. (2021) The Coaches' Handbook, Routledge, UK
17. Leary-Joyce, J. & Lines, H. (2018) Systemic Team Coaching, AoEC Press, UK
18 & 19. Widdowson & Barbour (2021) in Passmore, P. (2021) The Coaches' Handbook, Routledge, UK

The Transformative Domain

Transformative domain definition:

A skilful dialogic partnership in a co-created, reflective and experimental space that encourages engagement, development and learning[1].

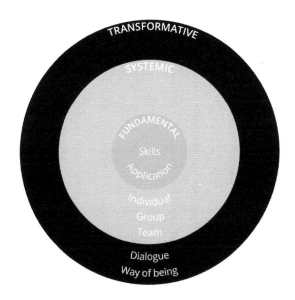

In the Transformative domain, we recognise the limitations of models-based coaching and educational systems as a whole. We collapse hierarchy to focus on the functioning of social networks. This is about developing a coaching presence and 'being' rather than a methodology. As previously discussed, in terms of the coaching spectrum and approach, the first two domains place the focus on two things: the belief that the coachee has all the answers (coaching), and the belief that the coach has the answers (mentoring). The diagram above shows the three core domains and their subdomains. The spectrum of the first two domains can, however, be limiting.

Hetty Einzig[2] talks about coaching as a profession at a crossroads. Do we continue down the road of more models and techniques and become ever more brilliant technicians or do we aspire to be master craftsmen, more in tune with an artist? By progressing into the Transformative domain you begin to let go of conditioned coaching tendencies to become an artist.

People who progress to the Transformative domain engage with a deeper purpose as we will discover. You will not reach the Transformative domain without the knowledge and expertise found in the previous domains. The Fundamental and Systemic domains are therefore an apprenticeship into the mastery of the Transformative domain.

In this domain we can begin to move beyond transactional models, goals and solutions to a deeper transformative dialogic agenda. Transformative coaching takes into consideration the multifaceted context of educational settings rather than a linear outlook focussed on the individual or system. It is about being fluid and agile not solid and rigid in approach. Agility allows for space and creativity to happen.

As a coach in this domain you can provide direction for the conversation and ensure progress is made by entering their own experiences into the dialogue[3]. Coaching in the Transformative domain then challenges the orthodoxy, and indeed the fiction, of impartiality in a coaching partnership[4]. Your challenge is how to act with principle: drawing out internal values from the coachee, in the context of our own self-knowledge, rather than risk unconsciously imposing your own when unwanted[5].

I would say that working in the Transformative domain requires you, to a certain extent, to unlearn what you have learnt from coaching in the Fundamental and Systemic domains whilst also drawing on the array of skills you gained within them. A paradox if ever there was one!

Essentially, ensure you hold skills and approaches lightly when working in the Transformative domain. It can require a longer phase in the development of a coaching partnership, which naturally takes place over a period of time, to realistically engender the trust required to delve deeper into themes.

The Transformative domain has two subdomains:

- dialogue
- way of being

Dialogue

Dialogue is a particular type of conversation. When we engage in dialogue, we come prepared to do two things:

1. Listen without prejudice to what the other person is saying, suspending our convictions, opinions and beliefs
2. Say what needs to be said, respectfully

Dialogue is not the same as skilled conversation. Skilled conversation is the coming together of people with an agenda. A meeting of any type is a good example of this. Skilled conversation tends to be about negotiation and compromise. Often, little new arises from skilled conversation[6]. Trusting the dialogue to do its work can mean at times feeling apprehensive about potential turbulence and discomfort – this is always possible in an open, undirected and unfettered space. It can also create an atmosphere of anticipation and expectation[7].

Let go of the reins, adopt an open mindset and accept that you do not know the direction in which the coaching may go. This is a real strength as it allows new ideas and opinions to surface.

In this section we will explore:

- advocacy and enquiry
- developing fruitful dialogue
- the space between
- grounding
- using nature to become more present

Advocacy and enquiry

Amanda Ridings[8] talks about setting the scene for dialogue and explores the balance in conversation as two elements:

- advocacy
- inquiry

Advocacy

Advocacy is speaking what you think, speaking from a point of view. When done well this is concerned with offering direction and opinion and develops performance. When overdone advocacy can impose opinions and become forceful.

Inquiry

Inquiry is looking into what you do not yet know, what you do not yet understand. Inquiry involves holding ambiguity, difference and uncertainty and rummaging around in them for fresh connections, for new information or insights.

When done well this helps build on ideas and create new perspectives; done weakly it can be too passive and avoid facing issues head on.

When you recall a recent meeting, lesson or interaction consider the balance of conversation; I would hazard that most of us will have spent more time in the advocacy element as opposed to the inquiry.

I invite you to be curious and inquire more often.

Developing fruitful dialogue

We need then to strike a good balance between advocacy and inquiry. By doing this we can then develop 'fruitful dialogue' [9]. I like to think of it as a coming together, a communion of sorts.

Issacs[10] suggests there are five dimensions you as a coach can leverage to create the right conditions for dialogue:

1. Evoke the ideal

Ensure that dialogue has meaning and purpose without necessarily being about goals and targets (as it was in the Fundamental domain). Trust that something new and exciting will emerge from the interaction. Education can be obsessed with targets so be mindful of this potential bias!

2. Support dreaming out loud

Create a space where people can feel safe to offer unguarded contributions.

3. Deepen the listening

Check for listening and ensure people are providing opportunity for dialogue. Revisit the listening skills model in the Fundamental domain for 'intention' and 'identify'; listen for what others want to say and who people are.

4. Make it safe for opposers

Ensure that people feel safe to offer counter arguments in a respectful way. Take the personal side out of it.

5. Dare to suspend

To what extent do people suspend their tendency to defend their corner and open up to new possibilities and perspectives? This is moving from advocacy to inquiry.

These five dimensions are particularly relevant to group and team sessions of coaching as well as training. They also make great team contracting sessions at the start of a new academic year for example, setting the foundations for how the team will work going forward.

Personally, I find the critical dimension in promoting effective dialogue is in creating a space where people can feel safe. Psychological safety is an area we will explore further in a coaching way of leading (Part 3). You will need to develop your ability to work in this dialogic space, through being present to witness what is unfolding before you, which we will explore next.

Accessing 'the space between'

The space between' is full of ideas articulated in symbolic forms: inventions, questions, theories, books, music, art, science and maths. In this space we articulate and share our experiences of the world [11]*.* This is illustrated in the diagram below[12].

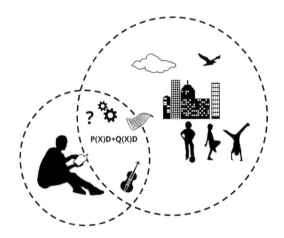

In coaching you cannot push change, you have to create the space for it to happen. This is a further development of the 'holding' concept outlined in the Fundamental and Systemic domains. In relation to coaching I think of this as a 'space between' which is a world between ourselves and what is not ourselves, what we know and don't know and what we are aware of and not aware of[13].

In the Transformative domain, through skilled dialogue we can invite our coachees to work with us in this space between, articulating and sharing experiences of the world.

According to Silverthorne[14] 'here is a space of trade and barter where stories are exchanged, secrets divulged, needs laid bare. There can be tears, great vulnerability; there can be compassion and great care.'

This is where effective dialogue comes in, working in a space that is co-created and emergent not pre-arranged and fixed.

There are parallels here with mindfulness and Buddhism. Awareness is slightly different to mindfulness in that we still make judgments and decisions, but there are skills found in both practices. Once you unlock the self-awareness found in meditation practices it can allow you to unlearn patterns, to be present and non-judgmental with what is unfolding in your coaching.

Grounding

Being able to ground yourself can be a way into developing awareness in the present moment, allowing you to create and work in a 'space between'.

Paul Wilson[15] has been called the 'guru of calm' and teaches meditation around the world. In his book *The Quiet* he talks about three steps you can take to change your focus from the day-to-day world to a more aware state:

- centre
- widen
- listen

The steps involve settling the mind and creating an inner stillness, so changing your state of consciousness. This can have benefits for grounding when you are stressed as well as for setting the scene prior to engaging in coaching sessions and dialogue.

Centre

The three phases to centre: forcefully breathe out, ground the body through your feet whether standing or sitting, and centre the spine by ensuring it is upright.

Widen

Relax your eyes and try fixing your gaze on one point to allow your peripheral vision to widen. This begins to involve your other senses and encourages seeing the bigger picture.

Listen

Finding the underlying quiet 'behind' everyday sounds is a grounding skill that you cannot force but rather cultivate over time. It is there all of the time and it requires you to relinquish preconceptions and preoccupations. Wilson visualises the layers involved with accessing 'the quiet' as illustrated below[16].

When you ground yourself through a technique such as centre, widen and listen you can begin to observe patterns in yourself, the way you interact with people around you, and in others. This in turn can heighten your ability to decipher dialogue and become a more intuitive coach.

I use this technique before most coaching sessions whether individual, group or team. When I reflect on my most effective coaching sessions they have occurred when I have been grounded and present. Grounding is also beneficial for taking time out of a situation, stepping back with order and control, whilst still participating. I regularly refer to grounding in my work with trainee teachers, in relation to behaviour management in the classroom. There is nothing to be gained from being too close to a situation and losing your temper.

If you have the ability to conjure an inner space of stillness you can engage in robust instruction without being overwhelmed or losing control.

Tapping into stillness and quiet will allow you, as a coach, to create a space to facilitate impactful dialogue. You will begin to hear what is really being said, and listen for what others want to say as well as who they are. This process once again aligns with the four stages of listening outlined in the Fundamental domain[17].

Breathing

An alternative way to ground yourself is through the deceptively simple breathing technique described by the famous Buddhist teacher, Tich Naht Hanh[18]:

As you are breathing in, simply say to yourself, "Breathing in, I know I am breathing in."

And as you exhale, say to yourself, "Breathing out, I know I am breathing out."

I remember trying this when first starting to develop mindfulness and found it so simple yet so difficult to do! If this is the case then begin with the centre, widen, listen process. The key is to be able to ground yourself in whatever way works best for you.

Using nature to become more present

In the modern world it is easy to lose sight of how nature can influence our perspective on life. Our separation from nature increases physical, emotional, mental and spiritual disease. Our connection with nature positively boosts these elements as well as enhancing our societal health[19].

We are generally taught that a coaching session should happen in the work environment and should be face-to-face so that you can read body language as well as keeping eye contact to ensure and reassure that you are listening. Whilst such a location provides an effective setting for coaching, over the years I have found real benefit from being more creative in where and when I coach. I frequently coach on the move, whilst walking, in a café or somewhere away from the day-to-day challenges.

It is a truism that a change of scene encourages a different perspective. Coach and coachee walking side by side in an informal setting, for example, can promote moving through issues and allows opportunities to open up. In a recent study, walking was found to release tension and to create creativity in a coaching interaction[20]. The action of walking raises awareness of your body, resulting in a degree of presence in the moment that will advance effective dialogue.

Peter Hawkins[21] takes this further and endorses letting the wider ecology do the coaching for you. He suggests taking some time in nature – or wherever you feel comfortable being outside – to really be present, open and uncluttered.

I find it valuable to reflect on the questions Hawkins poses to gain an understanding of how nature can help shape us and our coaching.

Lightly hold the question:

What can the wider ecology teach me about how to coach?" and allow yourself to wander and wait for whatever surprising answers may unfold. After a while the question may change to: "How can I help you, the wider ecology, do most of the coaching? [22]

In terms of coaching location, I find that a flexible and blended approach works well. In practice, this might mean meeting in person at a place of work, alongside walking coaching sessions and the flexibility to transition online when schedules and travel demand. For other coachees our coaching sessions will be fully online, for example when international travel is difficult. Then again, I have held coaching sessions at a coachee's home and have been introduced to their family; I have also coached on a train and an aeroplane!

Remember to discuss the flexibility and benefits of location options at the contracting stage with your coachee, to agree what is possible and appropriate.

Way of Being

In Fundamental and Systemic coaching we primarily address what the coachee is doing, separate from how they are being. As explored in Part 1 (Chapters 1 and 2), this is done through problem solving, goal setting and improving performance.

In the Transformative coaching domain, a person's 'way of being', or presence in the world, that is who they are, is the focus.

In coaching transformation occurs when the presence of the person is addressed[23]. This concept of 'being' can be difficult to describe but essentially it is an underlying feeling of mastery in your coaching that gives significance to your work; it is the second Transformative subdomain.

Attaining this transformation is about you having a coaching philosophy, not necessarily a model to implement. It is the principles and purpose of how you coach that matter rather than being fixated on a system or model[24]. It requires the integration of who you are as a person with who you are as a coach.

We will explore identity in Part 3 which very much aligns to this transformation. In coaching some call it a 'way of being'[25] or perhaps your signature presence[26].

The first step in this Transformative subdomain is to take some time to reflect on what defines you as a coach. The 'three Ps of coaching' process can be a helpful way to frame this deeper self-reflection[27].

Defining yourself as a coach – the Three Ps

1. What's your coaching philosophy?

Consider what are your go-to coaching models, coaching skills and approaches. Also think about the settings in which you coach.

2. Why do you coach? What is the purpose?

Consider what your aim is by coaching, for example, it might be to elevate the standards and efficacy of teaching practice in your setting, or perhaps to support the development of newly qualified teachers or aspiring leaders.

3. What is your process?

Do you operate firmly in the Fundamental domain, or perhaps you coach with other systems in mind? How do you set up the coaching partnership in terms of contracting?

Tip:

If you already have a coaching team set up in your school, then the three Ps can form an effective reflective session on your collective practice and your coaching identity.

Exploring your characteristics as a coach – your Way of Being

Lucy Widdowson and Paul Barbour[28] outline four characteristics of a coach's way of being that support the development of your coaching practice: connection, confidence, courage and continuing:

Connection

It could be argued that this is the most important part of the coaching partnership: building trust and creating a space where people feel safe to explore issues. This links to holding, as previously outlined, as well as the space between.

Confidence

This involves being confident in your own coaching ability but avoiding over confidence or egotistical behaviour. This comes from experience and through coaching in a range of settings.

Courage

As a coach you need to have the confidence to be flexible in your approach and continue to be present when in uncomfortable situations. If something isn't working in the coaching then let it go and adapt accordingly. Have the courage to ask the question that needs asking to allow themes to be explored. Being comfortable with silence in a coaching conversation is also important.

Continuing

To be an effective coach demands an openness to learning and development of your coaching, including asking for support when necessary. This includes coaching supervision and potential accreditation.

Coaching flow

As you progress through the coaching domains, your 'way of doing' – that is understanding and competency of coaching skills and approaches – develops.

You will find that your 'way of being' develops alongside your 'way of doing', as the diagram overleaf demonstrates (adapted from the 'being, doing and knowing' model of team coaching development by Widdowson and Barbour[28]).

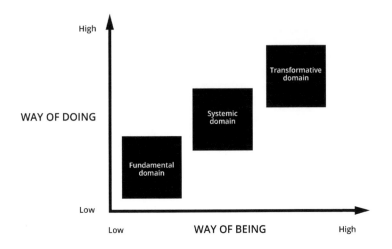

Over time you will develop a coaching way of being that is aligned to a highly effective coaching level of doing; this is the sweet spot, referred to as 'flow'. Flow is characterised by a strong sense of internal integration, high levels of attention and concentration and at times a complete loss of self-awareness[30].

I believe that coaching 'flow' is ignited when you are coaching in a transformative way; an expressive state that might be described as uplifting and transcendental. Simply holding a coaching space is not sufficient to transform on its own. Flow experiences require participation and co-creation, key elements of the Transformative coaching domain.

We will also explore co-creation in Part 2, a coaching way of teaching.

When to use a Transformative coaching approach?

The Transformative approach fits incredibly well within a new era of complexity in education, where people are looking to align the personal with the professional.

- Incorporate dialogue and way of being when working across each of the domains, whether a models-based approach or more widely
- Implement when engaged in all interactions in your setting to support a coaching culture

Limitations of the Transformative domain

- In education settings when do we get enough time to linger in dialogue?
- Getting people to this level takes time and resource
- Is this delving too deep for some? It could be argued that people don't want to open up at work, for example
- Developing the conditions for reflections and awareness can be challenging in busy schedules

Summary

- Two subdomains: dialogue and way of being
- Creating the conditions conducive to dialogue
- Forms of dialogue: advocacy, inquiry, fruitful dialogue
- Accessing the space between, grounding, breathing, becoming more present
- Coaching presence: defining yourself as a coach, your coaching characteristics, coaching flow

References

1. McKie, N. (2021), All Ways Coaching, Cadogan Press, UK
2. Einzig, H. (2017) The Future of Coaching, Routledge, UK
3. Stelter, R. (2019) The Art of Dialogue in Coaching, Routledge, UK
4 & 5. Einzig, H. (2017) The Future of Coaching, Routledge, UK
6 Lawrence, P. (2020) Dialogue, Coaching and Change, Centre for Coaching in Organisations, Australia
7. Armstrong, H. (2012) in Passmore, P. (2021) The Coaches' Handbook, Routledge, UK
8. Ridings, A. (2011) Pause For Breath, Live It Publishing, UK
9. Stelter, R. (2019) The Art of Dialogue in Coaching, Routledge, UK
10. Issacs, W (1999) in Lawrence, P., Hill, S., Priestland, A., Forrestal, C., Rommerts, F., Hyslop, I. & Manning, M. (2019) The Tao of Dialogue, Routledge Focus, UK
11. Swanwick, K. (1999) Teaching Music Musically, Routledge Falmer, UK
12. Diagram adapted from Swanwick, K. (1999), Teaching Music Musically, Routledge Falmer, UK
13. Swanwick, K. (1999) Teaching Music Musically, Routledge Falmer, UK
14. Silverthorne, G. (2021), (www.takumix.org/the-intimate-space-between-two-people/)
15 & 16. Wilson, P. (2006) The Quiet, MacMillan, UK
17. Lawrence, P., Hill, S., Priestland, A., Forrestal, C., Rommerts, F., Hyslop, I. & Manning, M. (2019) The Tao of Dialogue, Routledge Focus, UK
18. Tich Naht Hanh (2001) You Are Here, Shambhala, US
19. Strozzi-Heckler, R. (2014) The Art of Somatic Coaching, North Atlantic Books, US
20. Jones, R. (2021) Coaching Academic Podcast referring to Cook, S. & Van Nieuwerburgh, C. (2020) The Experience of Coaching Whilst Walking: A Pilot Study, The Coaching Psychologist, 156(2)
21 & 22. Hawkins, P. (2020) (www.renewalassociates.co.uk/2020/11/let-the-wider-ecology-do-the-coaching/)
23. Strozzi-Heckler, R. (2014) The Art of Somatic Coaching, North Atlantic Books, US
24. Rogers, B. (2021) Talent Takes Practice podcast, BBC, UK
25. Campbell, J. & Van Nieuwerburgh, C. (2018) The Leader's Guide to Coaching in Schools, Corwin Press, London
26. Einzig, H. (2017) The Future of Coaching, Routledge, UK
27. Jackson, P. & Bachkirova, T. in P3 (Centre for Coaching in Organisations) in Lawrence, P. Becoming A Systemic Coach white paper, Feb 2020
28. Widdowson, L. & Barbour, P. (2021) Building High Performing Teams, KognaPage, UK
29. Diagram adapted from Widdowson, L. & Barbour, P. (2021) Building High Performing Teams, KognaPage, UK
30. Swanwick, K. (1999) Teaching Music Musically, Routledge Falmer, UK

Integration: Putting It All Together

Your journey through the three domains accomplishes your coaching evolution. In the Fundamental domain your coaching develops through skills acquisition and the beginnings of establishing your coaching presence, using the materials available to you.

In the Systemic domain your coaching gains the capacity for wider reach. You begin to work in groups and teams. It is through this work and experience that coaching presence continues to mature and achieve wider impact.

In the Transformative domain your way of coaching advances in parallel with an ability to foster your way of being. Dialogue becomes important as you move past purely model-based approaches. This is where the real significance and value of coaching can be seen.

Now let us explore how we can combine domains to enact a culture of coaching in your setting.

Creating a Coaching Culture

Culture is everything that glues an organisation together. It includes elements such as norms of purpose, values, ethos and approach – aspects of the environment and atmosphere that can be perceived as difficult to evaluate, measure and therefore manage. When visiting schools, I find you can walk in and know immediately whether this is a place you want to be or not. This 'invisibility' causes some people to treat culture as a soft topic in the same way they do coaching, but it is the core that determines how we get things done[1].

Central features of a school culture are[2]:

- a focus on the values and beliefs of member of the organisation
- emphasis on the development of shared norms and meaning
- expressed through rituals and ceremonies

Coaching culture

I hear a lot about schools and educational institutions having a 'coaching culture', which in reality usually consists of pockets of one-to-one coaching rather than shared norms and beliefs. To truly achieve a highly effective coaching culture a multi-disciplinary approach is required, fusing and activating all the coaching domains.

A coaching culture is a setting in which coaching is the predominant style of management and teamwork, and where commitment to grow the organisation is embedded in a parallel commitment to grow the people in the organisation[3].

If you favour one coaching domain more than others this brings imbalance. Only by engaging all stakeholders through all domains can you get the full integration that leads to a coaching culture, as illustrated in the diagram opposite. This process can take time, but I would say that once the framework is set up in the right way things can move forward at a manageable pace.

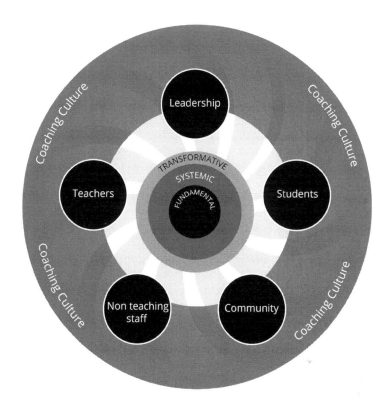

Practical application: activating the domains at your school

How do you begin to activate each of the coaching domains within your educational setting? I have outlined examples of my own experience that can be adopted to get you started. As ever, you will need to make it work for your own particular setting and context.

Earmarking and ring-fencing dedicated time for these approaches in schools can be difficult, potentially necessitating some collaboration with outside coaching specialists and expertise to ensure implementation and impact. My advice is to get the right people involved from the off.

Activating the Fundamental domain

To start any coaching project or initiative you need to introduce and implement whole community training on the Fundamental domain coaching skills.

This can be done across a series of INSET sessions with time for self-directed learning where necessary. This really lays a solid foundation from which to develop your coaching practice.

As previously mentioned, do not introduce models before you develop skills.

Leadership

- Middle and senior leaders begin to use coaching skills and models in performance development conversations
- Coaching skills are used through interactions across roles, including meetings.
- Coaching models to be used to restructure meetings (explained in Part 3)
- Formal lesson observations are supplemented with walkthroughs, instructional coaching, unseen observations and incremental coaching approaches

Teachers

- All teachers engage with coaching conversations both formally and informally across their setting whether student facing, staff facing or external
- Lesson observations/walkthroughs have a coaching focus based around the implementation of coaching skills in lessons
- Teachers begin to incorporate fundamental coaching skills in classrooms to be explored in more depth in a coaching way of teaching
- Peer-to-peer coaching is happening across the school incorporating models

Students

- Students begin to use coaching methodology in lessons and school-wide
- Student leadership opportunities use Fundamental coaching approaches through buddying systems and in student-student meetings
- Students begin to peer teach each other using coaching skills in class
- Student committees use coaching models to structure meetings

Non-teaching staff

- Operational and administrative teams engage with coaching approaches across their roles including in meetings and interactions with all stakeholders
- They begin to use coaching skills and models in performance development conversations

Community

- Awareness of the coaching approach is raised among the wider school /organisation community with opportunities for specific coaching fundamentals training
- Parents begin to use a coaching approach to support their children at home as well as in parent groups and committees

Activating the Systemic domain

Leadership

- School leaders receive individual systemic coaching, including mapping, to further develop understanding of their roles. This might include exploring challenges from both a professional and personal perspective.

- Leadership groups receive group and team coaching to develop expertise in their particular area and set targets for overall improvement

Teachers

- Teaching staff, including heads of departments or phases, receive group coaching through action learning sets, further enhancing shared understanding across their setting as well as developing and supporting each other with contextual challenges
- Departments receive team coaching to develop expertise in their particular area and set targets for overall improvement planning
- Departments begin to take more ownership of their development and direction through team coaching programmes

Students

- Form or class groups receive group coaching to support the sharing of best practice, the setting of targets and overall planning in their work
- Team coaching for student leadership teams to set objectives and establish developmental targets

Non-teaching staff

- Mirroring teachers, non-teaching staff receive group coaching through action learning sets, further enhancing shared understanding across their setting as well as developing and supporting each other with context challenges
- Non-teaching staff are included in coaching programmes with other school stakeholders
- Departments receive team coaching to develop expertise in their particular area and set targets for overall improvement planning

Community

- The wider school or organisation community is engaged through facilitated group coaching of, for example, parent groups discussing how best to support their children
- Team coaching for governing boards and parent committees will enable the setting of objectives and establishment of improvement planning

Activating the Transformative domain

- Activation of the Transformative domain will gradually evolve through all stakeholders' advancement and implementation of their Fundamental and Systemic coaching expertise
- Coaching is the default leadership approach
- Leaders have access to trained coaches whether external or internal
- All staff have access to trained internal coaches from the trained coaching group (see below, how to get it to work)
- Coaching is a key element of staff induction processes
- Coaching is happening at all levels both in formal and informal contexts across all interactions and all levels. There is effective and meaningful dialogue in all interactions that develops shared understanding and learning
- Teacher and student recruitment procedures are underpinned by coaching methodology
- Over time there will be decreased reliance on Fundamental coaching skills and models (and indeed the domain hierarchy itself) as stakeholders transition to a more dialogue-based agenda
- There will be deeper connections and more in-depth understanding and awareness of individuals' way of being that will support each person's professional life and transcend the work environment
- People feel they belong and are supported

Further options

Interestingly, current coaching research identifies some evidence that younger coaches are more effective than older ones because young and relatively inexperienced coaches are less likely to be directive[4]. This brings up possibilities such as students coaching teachers which, although appearing to be a radical step, could be effective if students have the requisite coaching skills.

This could centre on how effective lessons are and potential reflections around pedagogy, framed around an agreed coaching model utilising Fundamental domain coaching skills. I think the bigger issue would be teachers' openness to being coached by students. Student voice is not always powerful in schools so this could be an effective way of developing this element.

The same approach could also encapsulate early career teachers coaching the more experienced members of staff. Feedback from the work I do with initial teacher training supports the notion that teachers newer to the profession can be more effective coaches and mentors to trainee teachers. There are power dynamics at play here but also opportunities to develop coaching across your setting.

Getting it to work in your school

I would argue that finding an education institution with a fully embedded and effective coaching culture is extremely rare. Reasons for this might include[5]:

- lack of clarity of purpose for the coaching
- coaching is not aligned with the organisation's improvement strategy
- varying quality of coaches and their coaching knowledge
- lack of impact due to misunderstanding of coaching approaches and skills, including specific contracting at the beginning
- lack of support – for both coaches and coaches across the organisation
- lack of evaluation of impact

In schools it sometimes feels like coaching can be a tick box exercise to promote wellbeing or to evidence school-wide collaboration. In the same way that mechanisms for success are put in place across other areas of school to drive improvement, so the correct infrastructure must be in place for a school's coaching culture to succeed. I have witnessed a number of schools attempting to set up an impactful coaching project without first creating the right conditions for coaching to take place effectively.

A common example is a school having a one-off coaching training session for staff without plans in place to monitor and continue learning. Another example is middle leaders receiving coaching but not senior leaders, so approaches become fragmented and frustrations kick in.

With this in mind, there are three pillars essential to building an effective and successful coaching culture in an educational setting[6]:

- a strong coaching steering group
- a trained coaching group
- a community of practice

Strong coaching steering group

The first essential pillar is the creation of a coaching steering group that has ownership of the coaching strategy, resources and review processes. The coaching strategy should closely align with the values, mission and development plans of the institution. For example, consider whether coaching is referred to in student admissions, staff recruitment, teaching and learning methodologies, and by pastoral and leadership teams.

The journey to embedding a coaching culture must be actively supported and engaged with by senior leaders, this is crucial. Ideally the steering group is formed through collaboration, with buy-in from stakeholders representing all parts of the organisation, not simply teachers. This steering group should have sufficient seniority and autonomy to make decisions, with good knowledge of the three coaching domains.

Developing a coaching strategy

Peter Hawkin's fishbone diagram[7] (adapted below) has proved very helpful to the groups and teams I work with in developing a coaching strategy. Its clarity makes it the perfect focus for an INSET session and a clear framework that the steering group can use to plan coaching development.

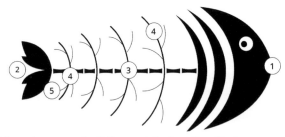

The 'fishbone' strategy building activity has five distinct steps:

1. Your institution's strategic coaching goals (the vision)

This could be along the lines of enhancing the quality of relationships and communication through coaching practices.
Or:
Creating new approaches to developing coaching in lessons, removing the barriers to innovative coaching practice.
Or:
Develop and enhance sector-leading coaching opportunities for all staff.

2. The current coaching state (where are we currently at?)

This could be coaching methodology in performance management processes
Or:
One-to-one coaching as part of lesson observations

Or:
Using coaching models in team meetings.

3. Agreed steps to take you from your current coaching state to your desired strategic goals, along a timeline from the 'tail' to the 'head'

This could be planned training, time set aside including timetabling or engagement with other schools.

4. The coaching activities required to be developed

Once the first three stages of the 'fishbone' are in place and agreed by your team, it is beneficial to break into groups to plan each of the coaching activities. As educationalists we are well versed in planning! Think of this as a lesson plan. There is plenty of scope and flexibility here in terms of how you structure the process. This is an excellent example of an activity within Stage 3 of the Systemic team coaching stages, for co-design coaching (see Part 1, Chapter 2).

5. The key ingredients of each coaching activity

What are the targets and resources needed to enable you to effectively develop coaching?

Trained coaching group

The second pillar of building a coaching culture is the creation of a trained coaching group who can train and develop staff within your institution. This group needs, as a minimum, an awareness of the coaching skills and approaches found in the Fundamental domain. You could also look at getting people certified through associations such as the International Coaching Federation (ICF)[8].

Individuals in the trained coaching group can also be members of the steering group but will need to ensure all coaching activities are aligned to the organisation's overall coaching strategy. Understanding how professional coaching can support teacher leadership, professional development and wellbeing is key.

The focus of the trained coaching group is on developing your organisation's coaching capacity. Consider combination coaching; making use of coaches with differing skill sets to further enhance effectiveness.

For example, both wellness and leadership coaches can work with staff to promote healthy performance. Remember that it may also be beneficial to use an external coach and expertise in tandem with your own trained coaching group.

You can also use the team coaching process outlined in the Systemic coaching domain to structure development. For example, each member of the steering group receives coaching and then themes are fed back in to reflect on overview training need.

Community of practice

A community of practice refers to a group of people who share a concern or a passion for something that they do and who interact regularly to learn how to do it better[9]. This occurs when people across an organisation buy into the idea of creating a coaching culture, with collaboration happening at all levels and across department, function or hierarchical boundaries. The goal in a community of practice is for coaching to be 'the way things are done' in your setting.

CollectivED: The Centre for Mentoring, Coaching & Professional Learning[10] is a research and practice centre based in The Carnegie School of Education in the UK and a great starting point for ideas on coaching in education. Action research projects where coaching initiatives are formed and tracked are another way to develop coaching.

To start with, aim for a small number of very significant and deep coaching research projects. These could encompass the impact of coaching skills in teaching, appraisals, peer-to-peer development as well as an overview of staff satisfaction and wellbeing. I like to think of these groups as co-enquiry study groups, sharing and keeping abreast of best practice. It is key to remain critical to ensure that coaching initiatives suit the context to which you are working.

Forming a Coaching Union

Once a coaching culture has been successfully established in your institution, what next? High performing schools and educational institutions are not islands. They see themselves as having a larger role in both a micro and macro sense[11]. It is possible to reach wider still and to develop what I term a 'coaching union'. This is where we begin to get relationships developing between schools that may be in the same region or across a trust or membership. The diagram below illustrates eight individual schools' coaching cultures working together to form a broader union.

Throughout my coaching practice, both internationally and domestically (I am based in the UK), I am always looking for opportunities to further expand and develop partnerships. I get a kick out of partnerships, being part of connecting people and schools to aid development. In terms of teaching, there are already great initiatives such as Jobs Alike Workshops (JAWS) by the Federation of British

International Schools In Asia (FOBISIA) in which subjects and roles are grouped for specific training across the Asia region.

I am encouraged by the idea of coaching unions, the forming of alliances across the world of education where no silos exist – whether in one school, a group of schools regionally, nationally or internationally.

In the Systemic domain, I referred to John Whittington's[12] idea of a peacock's tail, displaying multiple eyespots interlinked. When we combine coaching cultures from differing contexts we form our own eyespots. I have found that making connections across the education sector can bring confidence, shared understanding and learning to all involved. If we look further still across the international educational sector we can have further collaborations, as illustrated in the diagram below.

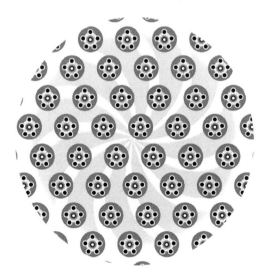

The opportunities and benefits that creating a union of coaching cultures brings are huge and extend far beyond what an individual school can achieve alone. Group coaching with headteachers from across the world allows the sharing of expertise and best practice.

Team coaching involving sector-leading policy makers can transform teaching practice and student outcomes.

Schools as beacons of coaching can deliver fundamental training and students coaching each other from different countries and regions sustains improved communication and takes international-mindedness to another level. Once we have union we can extend our ability to form partnerships, giving coaching a life of its own.

In the same way that a coaching culture cannot happen over the course of a couple of one-to-one sessions running in isolation, so having an isolated coaching culture in your setting without broader connection will not truly impact the wider educational sector.

Incremental Change

The key to your coaching evolution is to realise that change comes incrementally. It comes from training yourself to broaden your perspective so that you can grasp the complicated tangle of factors that shape any given situation and slowly transform your interactions with everything around you. Whilst having set goals can be beneficial, the pitfall is that that we will know our goal when we see it, thus limiting our development according to that truth[13]. Take your time at each stage and build in opportunities for reflection. Finally, have the courage to try different approaches. If you have an honest intention to help someone the likelihood is that you will.

The coaching context of education is diverse. Successfully launching and sustaining a coaching culture in your school (and beyond) is about fostering an integrative approach. As Part 1 of this book demonstrates, an awareness of each domain, their elements and when to utilise each one will influence the degree of real and sustainable impact. It is key to have a range of strategies at your disposal.

Coaching has the capacity to positively impact individuals across education, from CEOs and Vice-Chancellors to teachers, students, non-teaching staff and parent communities. Be in no doubt, it also has the capacity to transform the entire education sector. By widening our reach and enabling joined-up thinking it has the power to connect across the sector and have lasting, transformative effects.

References

1. Merchant, N. (2011) Culture Trumps Strategy Every Time (https://hbr-org.cdn.ampproject.org/c/s/hbr.org/amp/2011/03/culture-trumps-strategy-every)
2. Bush. T. (2011) Theories of Educational Leadership and Management, Sage, UK
3. Clutterbuck, D. (2018) How To Create a Coaching and Mentoring Culture in Your School, [PowerPoint presentation]
4. De Hann, E. (2021) Research Digest: What Can We Really Know About Our Coaching?, Coaching Today, April 2021
5 & 6 & 7. Adapted from Hawkins, P. (2012) Creating a Coaching Culture, McGraw Hill, UK
8. International Coaching Federation (ICF) www.coachingfederation.org
9. Chambers, M. (2021) (www.teamcoachinginternational.com/what-is-a-community-of-practice-why-should-i-join-one/)
10. CollectivED: The Centre for Mentoring, Coaching & Professional Learning (www.leedsbeckett.ac.uk/research/collectived/)
11. Buck, A. (2017) Leadership Matters, John Catt, UK
12. Whittington, J. (2020) System Coaching and Constellations, KoganPage, UK
13. Puett, M. & Gross-Loh, C. (2017) The Path, Penguin, UK

Part Two

A Coaching Way of Teaching

Formal education is not meeting the present or future needs of society, work or the environment. We still use an Industrial Age model to assess learning and we have not aligned curriculum goals with the true purpose of education[1]

The OECD (Organisation for Economic Co-Operation and Development) Learning Compass 2030 defines the knowledge, skills, attitudes and values that learners need to fulfil their potential and to contribute to the wellbeing of their communities and the planet. Student agency is a key element for 2030 and is rooted in the belief that students have the ability and the will to influence positively their own lives and the world around them. Student agency is defined as the capacity to set a goal, reflect and act responsibly to effect change, something very much aligned to the Fundamental coaching domain.

The current approach of most schools does not equip students with the skills and tools needed to succeed in the future. For example, in my work in coaching and training graduates into the financial and pharmaceutical industries the focus is frequently on developing the social and softer relational skills that companies perceive as lacking: 'Great knowledge, but can't work with others' is common feedback.

The same is true for the postgraduate teacher training courses I am involved with in which students can struggle with basic organisation and the development of relationships across schools and university.

Enacting a Coaching Way of Teaching

Coaching underpins the development of soft skills, managing change, ownership of learning, agility and the ability to work with ambiguity. These skills align with the coaching methods and approaches outlined in Part 1 and will also be explored in a coaching way of leading in Part 3. How then can education develop a coaching pedigree to support the potential reinvention of our schools to a 'people's age' of

education? A coaching way of teaching moves us on from the industrial and information age of education to an organic, model-based approach centred around people and purpose that incorporates the skills of effective coaching[2].

To enact a coaching way of teaching we will need to engage three approaches[3]:

- Formal: you are the teacher
- Non-formal: you are the facilitator
- Informal: you are the coach

In Part 2, Chapter 1 we will explore the formal teaching approach which I class as being the current status quo. You are the teacher. In Chapter 2 the non-formal teaching approach will take us to the edge of where we are collectively at as a teaching profession.

In this approach your role is more facilitating learning rather than purely teaching. In Chapter 3 the informal approach takes us firmly into new territory! You progress to being more of a coach, partnering with learners to support their development.

This framework of pedagogical approaches aligns with the evolution of a coaching repertoire as outlined in Part 1 (which will be referenced as we progress). When we fuse these three approaches to teaching with the three coaching domains outlined in Part 1, we have the coaching way of teaching, illustrated in the diagram opposite.

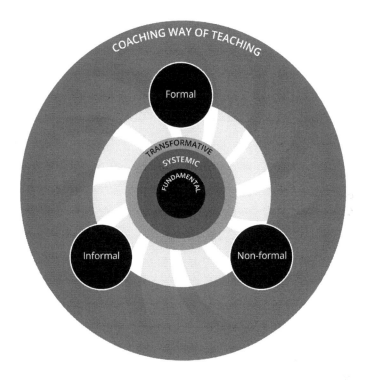

As in your coaching evolution, the three teaching approaches, whilst not a necessarily a progression, can be seen to provide a framework for focussing on the engagement of a range of learners. All approaches are of value. We will draw on your coaching evolution at every step and unpick how coaching can play a key part in the future of education.

Part Two: Chapter 1

A Formal Approach

Formal education is focussed on the procedural quality concept; that is, implementing systems and procedures in order to measure quality. 'Proving, approving and reporting are the key descriptors. It is an accountability or audit approach that is concerned to ensure consistency and conformity'[4]. This 'hard quality' approach places emphasis on the use of statistical methods to drive improvement [5]. In education these types of measurement include the publishing of examination results and league tables and also encapsulate the concept of 'performativity'. Performativity signifies an obsession with targets, league tables, audit, accountability and similar mechanisms of (managerial) control[6].

The above is true of the state education system in the UK. International education is often geared the same way and this is about cultural capital, local students getting access to different educational opportunities that they may not have had previously. Marketing and admissions materials for these schools promote the university destinations of their former students and the prestigious university careers and qualifications of their teaching staff.

I remember walking into a British international school in China many years ago on a scouting mission to support me setting up a sixth form for a similar school elsewhere in China. The first things I encountered as I walked in were university guidance for both UK and US colleges. I presumed these were simply for the older students but was told that a majority were for families with children currently in primary school looking at forging a road map into the top universities.

In a formal teaching setting students are inheritors of knowledge, values and practice, requiring basic skills that allow for an understanding of concepts and the passing of examinations. A formal teaching approach places the onus on the teacher to drive the learning process by informing and transmitting information directly to students in a traditional way. Formal assessment is undertaken individually assessing knowledge of curriculum. This is about the building of skills through whole class approaches, standardised teaching practices and organisation – some might say the 'stand and deliver' model of education. Green[7], drawing on research undertaken in Nordic countries argues that formal learning occurs when the activity is sequenced beforehand by a teacher or other leader who leads and manages the activity. This linear, sequenced planning is delivered in set timetables that are based around subjects and age ranges.

Most Singapore state schools are examples of a more traditional, performative education with a focus on curriculum coverage. There is an inclination for teachers to 'teach to the test', pragmatic, direct and instructional, focussing on drills, textbooks and worksheets and a preponderance for closed questions and limited exchanges[8].

The Chinese teaching style is also largely teacher-centred and sometimes described as a 'spoon-feed model'[9]. The UK education sector, from compulsory to higher education, also features strongly formal approaches, as is the case for most other nations around the world.

Coaching in Formal Teaching

In a coaching sense the formal approach aligns with being directive, giving advice and solving problems in a mentoring way. This is of course required at times, for students' comprehension and knowledge. However, the formal approach can be difficult to sell to students. Student engagement or lack thereof has been the persistent scourge of traditional education especially when children are forced to learn something that they do not see as relevant to them[10]. Young people find themselves described as 'human resources', to be moulded into a service they do not necessarily want. This can lead to passive reception, not engagement[11].

Teaching Fundamentals

As we have seen, coaching in the Fundamental domain requires you to get the basics in place, focussing on your coaching skills and models-based application. The same is true in relation to a formal teaching approach. The Fundamental domain coaching skill that I view as key in this formal approach is questioning, which transcends all teaching approaches.

Questioning

When starting school children are full of questions but formal approaches mean that teachers can be focussed on their pupils passing tests, by cramming as much information into lessons as possible. Questions from the class then get in the way of this march towards examinations. The questions that *are* asked are designed to test recall and keep students paying attention, if only from fear of being called on next[12].

We know from Barak Rosenshine[13] as part of his *Principles of Instruction* that by asking large numbers of questions and checking responses a teacher determines how well the material has been learned. Honing your Fundamental coaching skills is, in the same way, key to effective teaching.

Formal techniques include:

- targeted questioning, with no hands up, to ensure everyone has an opportunity to be asked and thus engaged
- think, pair and share is a classic questioning and feedback example and is particularly effective when learners are not engaging in whole class questioning

When observing teachers across a range of settings, I am struck by how questioning in particular is underplayed. Questioning allows you to guide practice and scaffold learning, which are other key elements of Rosenshine's work.

When observing trainee teachers for example, it is common to see them ask a question, not provide sufficient time for the class to answer and then answer the question themselves. Research has found that on average, a teacher spends one-third of their time questioning students[14].

Increasing the waiting time improves the number and quality of the responses: three seconds for a lower-order question and more than ten seconds for a higher-order question[15]. Leaning into the silence and giving students time to think is the key take-away here.

I also know, from my own experience when training to be a coach and developing my questioning, the huge impact that the way I question has through moments of teaching. 'For the teacher or coach, the question has to be how to give instructions in such a way as to help the natural learning process of the student and not interfere with it.'[16]

This of course is only possible when we begin to listen to students and give them space to answer. Listening as well as questioning weaves its way through all formal teaching approaches.

Coaching and Professional Standards

I will use the UK Teachers' Standards[17] as a benchmark to demonstrate how coaching can be utilised in a formal approach which you can adapt to your setting. (I have omitted Teacher Standard number 3 which is focussed on subject knowledge.)

Inspire, motivate and challenge

Teacher Standard number 1 is about setting high expectations which inspire, motivate and challenge students. In the same way in coaching, we also need to establish a safe and stimulating environment for pupils, rooted in mutual respect.

This has similarities with contracting in coaching. Utilising goal setting processes such as Polaris visioning and AIM SMART (outlined in the Fundamental coaching domain) can also help stretch and challenge pupils.

Promote progress and outcomes

In Teacher Standard 2 we look to guide pupils to reflect on their own progress and identify their emerging needs. This has parallels with the models application in the Fundamental domain: identify options and then formulate ways forward.

Plan and structure

Teacher Standard 4 is framed around planning and teaching well-structured lessons, from short term individual lesson plans for units to year-long schemes of work. In a formal teaching approach this involves setting lesson objectives and intentions using well known language such as:

- to enable...
- to develop an understanding of...
- to ensure that...
- to learn to...

It also involves outlining outcomes and success criteria using language such as:

- show understanding of...
- be able to...
- identify...
- evaluate...
- reflect on...

So, when planning, set up a group or team coaching space to reflect on the following questions:

- What is the curriculum we need to teach?
- What is the knowledge you want to teach to your students?

- How do you set targets?
- How do you assess progress in relation to targets?

Adaptability and differentiation

Teacher Standard 5 concentrates on adapting teaching to respond to the strengths of students. This is about differentiating your approach to enable students to progress and is the most difficult standard in my opinion. Being responsive to students requires you to have a toolkit of teaching strategies – this often comes with experience. I think of this as operating the Transformative coaching domain and choosing the coaching approach most aligned to the specific context. It necessitates knowledge and expertise of the Fundamental and Systemic domains.

Assessment and feedback

Teacher Standard 6 is concerned with accurate and productive use of assessment, giving students regular feedback and encouraging them to respond. In terms of feedback, in a formal teaching approach this should be designed to make students think, focus on learning goals and involve more work for the student than the teacher[18]. This has parallels in terms of coaching in the Fundamental domain with the coachee doing most of the talking whilst you listen. A classic example in teaching is the use of mini whiteboards to illicit feedback from a whole class to inform understanding.

Paul Black and Dylan Wiliam in their popular book *Inside the Black Box*[19] focus on the importance of being responsive in placing formative assessment at the heart of effective teaching. Discussion with the teacher provides the opportunity for the teacher to respond to and reorient a pupil's thinking. This is about the development of fruitful dialogue as explored in the Transformative coaching domain.

We also know from John Hattie and his *Visible Learning* research[20] that the most effective teachers create an optimal classroom climate for learning through developing trust as well as the importance of feedback. Hattie talks about teachers seeing learning through the eyes of students to help them become their own teachers. These elements will be discussed further in Part 3 but have huge parallels with developing an effective coaching partnership, empathy and empowerment.

Behaviour management

The managing of behaviour to create a climate for learning is a basic teaching skill – especially in the UK where there is continued focus on Teachers' Standard number 7: manage behaviour effectively to ensure a good and safe learning environment. In the same way that I see contracting as a much-underused element in coaching, the same can be said in terms of building a productive teaching environment.

It is vital for classroom teachers to have a systematic discipline plan that explains exactly what will happen when students choose to misbehave[21]. A systemic plan will cover 'what if' scenarios as well as regular contract reviews built in at the end of every lesson to supplement knowledge reviews.

An example of initial contracting questions could be:

- What would we expect to happen if we keep talking over each other in class?
- If we don't complete homework tasks what would we expect to happen?
- If you are late to lessons what will be the consequences?

In terms of reviews at the end of lessons:

- What behaviour do you feel was successful today?
- What elements of behaviour do we need on work on?
- If we improved our ability to listen to others what would be the impact?

Ask the students what behaviour we need to ensure a task is completed well,
e.g., 'listen' or 'respect each other's views'.

Once you have contracting in place, the key is to catch students' good behaviour: recognise and support them when they behave appropriately and let them know you like it, day in and day out[22].

This also has parallels with coaching in the championing of your coachee, seeing their best and supporting them through their journey. As a coach you can be close to your coachee but it is a different relationship to that of a friend.

Communicate effectively

A key element of Teacher Standard 8, fulfil wider professional responsibilities, is communicating effectively with stakeholders across your setting. This recalls the Transformative coaching domain in developing fruitful dialogue. In some of the parent and governor meetings I have been part of the idea of grounding was also applicable!

With the development of the Core Content Framework (CCF) and the forever changing Initial Teacher Training (ITT) inspection framework in play in the UK it is an interesting time to be working in the teacher training space. There is beginning to be more onus on holding the UK Teachers' Standards more lightly.

A number of ITT providers are beginning to introduce these standard benchmarks later in a teacher training course, after teaching has begun to develop rather than from the outset, to steer teaching progression.

In a coaching sense this is emblematic of moving on from a simple models-based approach to a fluid coaching agenda. As ever with teacher training it is the relationship between the trainee and school mentor that is key and this is where knowledge of fundamental coaching skills is so important.

Appraisals

Observations in a top-down format are part of the formal approach to teaching and this is needed at times. Your line manager observes you and provides feedback. I always ask myself if there is any value in continuous formal observations of teachers who are consistently good practitioners. Walk-throughs, instructional coaching and incremental coaching models (as outlined in the Fundamental coaching domain) can be more effective and there is a shift in perspective here with more schools going down this route.

Inspections are still carried out. I found the team inspecting I did for the Independent Schools Inspectorate enjoyable because there was at least some collaborative and developmental approach; as a serving senior school leader at the time I could empathise and understand current issues. This felt developmental rather than evaluative and as such this resulted in better buy-in from each school.

Summary

The premise of a formal teaching approach is control and structure. In terms of utilising your coaching skills, the formal approach is about finding opportunities to embed them across an existing curriculum in your setting.

- Teachers teach and drive the learning process by delivering and planning sequenced activities in a linear way
- Standards are the benchmark of teaching
- Students are inheritors of knowledge, teachers have the knowledge and content
- Understanding of knowledge is demonstrated individually
- Leverage Fundamental coaching skills to support your teaching basics such as contracting for behaviour, questioning, listening and feedback

References

1 & 2. Carpenter, R. (2020) A Tale of Two Ideologies, (www.robcarpenter.org.uk/44/climbing-the-hill/post/113/a-tale-of-two-ideologies-our-gutenberg-moment#)

3. Green, L. (2020) Musical Futures, UCL Institute of Education, London

4. Sallis, E. (2002 3rd Ed.) Total Quality Management in Education, Kogan Page Ltd, London

5. Keleman, M. (2003) Managing Quality, Sage, UK

6. Dent, M. & Whitehead, S. (2002) Managing Professional Identities, Keele University Tutor Notes, UK

7. Green, L. (2008) Music Informal Learning and The School, Ashgate Publishing, UK

8. Hogan, D., Towndrow, P., Kwek, D., Rahim, R., Chan, M. & Luo, S. (2014) in Pollard, A. (2014) Readings for Reflective Teaching in Schools, Bloomsbury, UK

9. Zhong, Z. (2013) in Hsieh, P. (2013) Education in East Asia, Bloomsbury, London

10. Zhao, Y. (2012) World Class Learners, Sage Publications, London, UK

11. Greene, M. (1995) Releasing The Imagination, Jossey-Bass, US

12. Gregersen, H. (2018) Questions Are The Answer, Harper Collins, US

13. Rosenshine, B. (2012) Principals of Instruction, American Educator, Spring 2012, (https://moodle.warwick.ac.uk/pluginfile.php/1530968/mod_book/chapter/100464/Principles%20of%20instruction%20Rosenshine-1.pdf)

14 & 15. Hastings, S. (2003) Questioning, TES Newspaper, 4 July, (www.tes.co.uk/article.aspx?storycode=381755)

16. Gallwey, T. (2015) The Inner Game of Tennis, Pan Publishing, UK

17. Department for Education (2011) UK Teacher's Standards, Crown, UK

18. Sherrington, T. & Caviglioli, O. (2020), Teaching Walkthrus, John Catt Educational Ltd, UK

19. Black, P. & Wiliam, D. (2010) Inside the Black Box: Raising Standards Through Classroom Assessment, GL assessment Limited, UK

20. Hattie, J. (2012) Visible Learning for Teachers: Maximising Impact on Learning, Routledge, UK

21 & 22. Canter, L. (2018) Assertive Discipline More Than Names on the Board and Marbles in a Jar (https://moodle.warwick.ac.uk/pluginfile.php/1183426/mod_book/chapter/80019/Assertive%20Discipline%20More%20Than%20Names%20on%20the%20Board%20and%20Marbles%20in%20a%20Jar%20-%20Lee%20Canter.pdf)

A Non-formal Approach

A non-formal teaching approach moves away from the idea of students as purely inheritors of information. Increased responsibility shifts onto the students. Essentially this is about negotiated facilitation, with students having increased ownership and control of the curriculum and activities being taught.

A non-formal approach encourages students to find their 'voice', express their ideas, opinions and concerns, and it is the obligation of teachers and fellow students to listen and treat them with due seriousness[1]. We are beginning to relinquish control and shift focus to social networks in alignment with the Systemic and Transformative coaching domains.

Coaching in Non-formal Teaching

In terms of coaching, the non-formal teaching approach can be associated with non-directive methodology, in which the teacher helps students to find their own solutions. There are also similarities with group and team coaching in terms of facilitation. In non-formal teaching the teacher still leads the learning but this is now co-constructed and adapted with and to the learners' needs. Co-creation is happening when staff and students work collaboratively with one another to create components of curricula and/or pedagogical approaches[2]. This is enhanced when the teacher and students share a language to describe different pedagogical approaches[3].

The idea of scaffolding activities is important here.

Example:

The teacher may start by establishing the lesson objectives before inviting students to decide the success criteria.

In subsequent lessons, students take more ownership of the actual lesson objectives alongside the success criteria.

Finland is a good example of a nation espousing a non-formal pedagogy. In the Finnish education system, there is development of a personal road map for learning, less focus on classroom-based teaching, the development of interpersonal skills and problem solving. Engagement and creativity are pointers of success, opposite to competition and testing approaches[4]. The benefits of this pedagogical method have been: increased engagement, motivation and improved teaching and learning experiences[5].

Stephen Cox, CEO at New Nordic School, talks about the teacher being an activator of learning; this is formed around a partnership between the teacher, student and technology. 'Everyone has a role with the teacher's role is being activating the deeper learning to take place around critical inquiry and thinking skills.'[6]

In this style of teaching and learning there is sensitivity around content that reflects the interests of both teacher and learners – the emphasis is on the teacher modelling skills rather than solving and advising. In an article forecasting future education trends, Nord Anglian schools group Chief Executive Andrew Fitzmaurice[7] predicts this 'crowdsourcing' approach will become more prevalent: 'What is taught in classrooms will be increasingly decided by pupils. They'll direct the exploration of subjects, drawing on topical issues affecting the world they live in, to inform questions and the development of discussions.' As such, the onus is placed on students and teachers need to become more aware of individuals. Identifying energy blocks, such as limiting beliefs (as outlined in the Fundamental coaching domain) around learning and coaching, becomes important.

As teachers, we are used to 'teaching' and as such it can be difficult to stop directly instructing; we need to get out of our own way. It is worth remembering that sometimes our interactions decrease the probability of someone understanding and improving – too much instruction can be worse than none at all[8]. It is the beginning of the promotion of dialogue, as explored in the Transformative coaching domain, as a way of learning.

Developing positive relationships

Developing positive relationships is a crucial aspect of non-formal teaching approaches and coaching. Relationships that are non-directive, empathic, warm and encourage thinking and learning have correlations with: increased participation, critical thinking, student satisfaction, perceived and actual achievement, self-esteem, positive motivation, social connection and attendance, low drop-out rates and reduction in disruptive behaviour[9].

Fostering positive relationships links with 'relational pedagogy' – it is something people develop as they have experiences with each other and the world around them[10]. Relational pedagogy argues the importance of developing meaningful relationships between students, their peers and teachers in order for effective learning to take place[11].You could say that this approach should underpin *all* teaching, as well as coaching, as it is about engagement and motivating people to achieve the best possible outcomes. Of course, there has to be a fine line drawn in terms of teacher-student relationships and safeguarding, however this all comes back to the ability to utilise your coaching evolution to good effect. Rather than direct instruction and delivery of a set curriculum, you can develop co-construction and active learning that includes students in the learning process itself.

Another way to think about developing positive relationships is through 'gratitude as a pedagogy' as outlined in the innovating *Pedagogy 2021* report from the Open University[12]. Gratitude can help students to improve the relationships with those around them in an academic context, and beyond. An example of this is asking teachers and students to stop and examine their attitude before commencing teaching and learning, as well as during learning activities. This can bring to light any negative attitudes towards different types of learning. The key is then to replace these with gratitude, to develop awareness and increase motivation. Gratitude as a pedagogy is similar to responsive formative assessment during teaching; the coaching equivalent is contracting and review.

The non-formal approach is present in the ten effective teaching and learning principles that are conceptualised by the UK's *Teaching and Learning Research Programme*[13] which gathered information from a number of studies over a 12-year period. Key principles include active engagement of the learners through promoting independence and autonomy, which we can see aligns with a non-directive Fundamental coaching approach. Fostering social processes with learners sharing ideas in a collaborative way is also a key theme in the teaching and learning principles, containing aspects of both the Systemic and Transformative domains[14]. So, for learners to have the confidence to take more ownership of their learning they need to develop positive relationships with their peers and their teacher through opportunities to collaborate and work towards shared goals[15].

The *Great Teaching Toolkit Evidence Review*[16] identifies tools and behaviours for teachers searching for ways to help their students' learning. It provides a credible summary of the elements of great teaching practice, the kind that impact most on learning. The creation of a supportive environment for learning, developing relationships and a climate for learning were found to be key. Coaching aligns very much with the idea of developing a space in which to hold agendas and fostering support.

Virtual teaching

The swift move to online teaching in schools across the world in 2020 was demanded by the circumstances in which so many schools found themselves. The prevalence of online teaching is unlikely to dissipate and so it is interesting to unpick the links to a non-formal teaching approach that can lend itself well to this teaching medium.

When developing online courses I find the blend of synchronous and asynchronous material is key. Synchronous, or 'live' learning is better when it is important to have thorough exchanges of perspectives among your students and when students are learning from each other. As the teacher, you are playing the facilitator or mediator role. Asynchronous, or 'not live' learning, is more effective when you want students to have an understanding of ideas before live sessions and when you want students to engage with material at their own pace. This combination provides greater flexibility for students to engage on their own terms and also take more ownership of the direction in which they take their learning.

Example 1:

1. Students engage with an article or piece of writing that is made available before the lesson.
2. They write a short reflection on this based around criteria previously agreed (or even co-constructed).
3. They come to the live online session ready to feedback their reflection with peers as a starter activity.
4. This then leads into an online reflective writing session with the teacher.

A variation:

1. Students are asked to engage with an article in pairs before the lesson.
2. They work together to prepare a short reflection.
3. They come to the live online session ready to feedback their reflection with peers as a starter activity.
4. This then leads into an online reflective writing session with the teacher.

Example 2:

1. Students engage with an article or piece of writing that is made available before the lesson.
2. They write a short reflection on an online discussion board set up by the teacher along with other members of the class.
3. Everyone provides peer feedback on one other student reflection (this could include the teacher).
4. The feedback is taken on board by students and adjustments made to their original reflection.

5. Students come to the live online session ready to feedback their reflection with peers as a starter activity.
6. This then leads into an online reflective writing session with the teacher.

Student learning can therefore be developed virtually by structuring opportunities for student interaction with teachers, the material to be learned, and their peers[18].

Connection is essential because the teacher engages in various forms of dialogue with remote students, including 'instructing, guiding, questioning, listening, assessing, advising, admonishing, and reassuring as appropriate'[19].

In this way, the 'remote' teacher acts as both facilitator and instructor incorporating elements of all coaching domains from Fundamental coaching skills to fruitful dialogue.

Facilitating class ownership

We will explore team coaching in more depth in Part 3, but in order to create a class set-up that facilitates more task ownership, whether face to face or virtually, you can use the following process[20]:

- Set a clear understanding of the student team's task. Contracting is once again important here in terms of students understanding their responsibilities.
- Build a strong teamworking environment through the monitoring of interactions and ensuring that any conflict between students is dealt with.
- Support individual students through individual goals and objectives. Depending on age these would be provided or set themselves.

In terms of setting up an environment to facilitate discussions, you can look to incorporate action learning sets from the Systemic domain depending on the age of students and your setting.

Students can take it in turns to bring challenges with coaching from others in the group. I have found this works well with debates and is a very collaborative way of learning, with the opportunity for learners to provide feedback to each other.

Example:

The most challenging elements of exam revision
- Students are formed into groups of six.
- One student in each team brings a revision challenge of their own.
- The other students in their team then take it in turns to ask questions and provide advice.
- The focus student takes the feedback on board and sets targets in light of the feedback.
- The next student brings their revision challenge to the table and the cycle continues.

Developing student ownership: Appreciative Enquiry

Appreciative Enquiry used in non-formal settings encourages exploration and enquiry as a process to develop and a way to ignite change.

There are five main principles of Appreciative Enquiry[21]:

1. Positive: positive questions drive change in a positive way
2. Constructivist: we construct understanding through effective conversation and dialogue
3. Poetic: things are expressed through a narrative, such as a poem or story, to engender creativity
4. Simultaneity: an openness to inquire to ignite change
5. Anticipatory: imagination drives action through visioning and goal setting

These principles can be applied to teaching as well as other contexts in both professional and personal life. You will see that there are coaching skills and approaches embedded at every stage, from questioning, dialogue to goal setting and forwarding the action.

This approach lends itself to co-creation and collaboration as found in the Transformative coaching domain, as well as the dialogic container outlined in Part 3.

According to Mohr & Magruder Watkins's *Roadmap for Creating Positive Futures*[22], there are five main steps to tackling a given issue within a framework of Appreciative Enquiry, and they can be adapted for students in the non-formal teaching approach.

1. Define: what is the desired outcome? This could be student learning objectives or co-created target setting.
2. Discovery: what are our strengths? Students deciphering their skills and knowledge that can be utilised for a given task or project.
3. Dream: what would work well in the future? This is about students being flexible in terms of responding to emergent changes in desired outcomes.
4. Design: what action would we need to make it happen? Creating actions to enact goals
5. Deploy: taking that action.

Philosophy for Children

Philosophy for Children or P4C is an ideology that builds on the Appreciative Enquiry concept and aligns to the non-formal teaching approach. It was established over 40 years ago by Professor Matthew Lipman of Montclair State University in the US[23]. In P4C, the process works as follows:

- A stimulus, such as a story, video clip or image, is shared with a group of children.
- The children are encouraged by a teacher to come up with big, engaging philosophical questions about the stimulus[24]. Examples could be: is it ever ok to lie? Do we all have the same rights?
- Typically, the children then vote or choose one of the questions they would like to explore and, supported by the teacher, begin to think more deeply and philosophically. This is encouraged

using the 4Cs of P4C: critical, creative, collaborative and caring thinking.

For the teacher, the third task in the process is very much about engaging the core coaching skills outlined in the Fundamental domain.

The P4C approach concerns promoting dialogue and a community of enquiry where there is a search for understanding, truth, meaning and values supported by reasoning[25]. This is very much aligned to the Transformative coaching domain, inviting others into the space between, a shared space for reflection where people can change and develop26.

P4C outcomes centre on[27]:

- Improved oral communication skills, literacy and numeracy, particularly for the less able
- Improved social and emotional development, and more collaborative relationships with others
- Improved articulacy and confidence in speaking and listening
- Students become more able to challenge and question, within the rules of respectful dialogue

The process also encourages students in starting to develop their own Fundamental coaching skills whilst also increasing their educational attainment.

International Teacher Training Curriculum Development

As part of the curriculum development planning for the Warwick PGCE international course we attended an engaging hands-on session, led by a superb academic technologist, which aligned to the community of enquiry concept highlighted in the P4C process. The main premise of this session was to enable us to identify the key principles of course delivery before we drilled down further into module content planning. The session was structured around the Arena Blended Connected (ABC) curriculum development model, used as a prism through which to craft reflections on our own curriculum development.

Arena Blended Connected

Created by UCL Digital Education, the ABC model[28] is a collaborative workshop in which a visual story board is produced to sequence learning activities, assessment and potential outcomes. Through this model different learning types are identified:

- Acquisition: listening to a lecture, reading books and watching demonstrations
- Collaboration: discussion, practice and production
- Discussion: articulation of ideas and questions
- Investigation: explore, compare and critique
- Practice: adapt actions to the task and use feedback for improvement
- Production: articulation of current understanding and how to apply this

The process started with mapping out how both the local (primary and secondary) and international PGCE programmes are/would be delivered in terms of the learning types, marking the frequency that each learning principle is used (see diagram below). The current (local) PGCE course was plotted by a grey line before mapping the proposed PGCE international course in black. We were then able to understand the difference in terms of delivery approach between the two sister courses, helping to inform our planning.

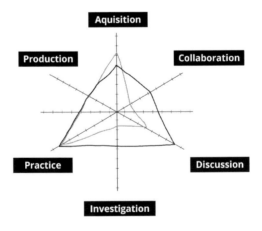

Local vs international

In terms of production and practice curriculum elements, we saw a close synergy between the local and international offerings. Assessed teaching practice is benchmarked against the UK Standards, and assessment points throughout the course along with Masters level assignments are compulsory components across the board.

In comparison to the international programme, we believed the local PGCE is slightly more acquisition focussed, mainly due to the increased university element including access to conferences and workshops across campus. This also covers virtual work.

In relation to the strengths of the proposed PGCE international course, we were looking at deeper expectations around collaboration, discussion and investigation. These elements would be promoted in terms of the face-to-face induction, online 'live' sessions and self-study preparation.

It was clear from the curriculum development session that the key pedagogical tenets of the PGCE international programme are centred on collaboration, discussion and investigation. Ensuring that these elements are woven through the module planning all became a key focus. Less acquisition, more collaboration, investigation and discussion are all hallmarks of coaching and more non-formal learning approaches.

Barriers to Non-formal Approaches

As you might imagine there are some barriers to students co-creating teaching and learning. These include:

- the need for students to have specific skills or expertise
- their involvement will steer the learning away from what was originally planned[29]
- in relation to 'crowdsourcing', while set examinations are in place across a majority of national and international education systems this can be difficult to implement

There is also a misconception that through a less formal approach chaos reigns. The belief exists that by holding learners to account for their actions and tasks in a more fluid approach, the teacher-learner relationship is disrupted. How many times have you swerved the opportunity to try something a little more 'out of the box' with your class in fear of a senior leader walking past and thinking things are out of control? I think this comes back to contracting, in terms of expectations around managing your class and the expectations of leaders within your setting.

It is important to curate an environment in your classroom that is high challenge and high trust. By outlining the behaviours that are desirable you can then hold learners accountable to them.

Summary

Coaching weaves its way through effective non-formal teaching whether face to face or virtual. Utilise your coaching skills: questioning, listening to understand, and creating space to allow discussion and dialogue. Develop your ability to empathise and acknowledge in order to build strong relationships in a trusting environment.

- Teachers co-create learning with students
- The role of facilitator rather than teacher
- Students have more ownership and control of the curriculum and activities being taught

References

1. Alexander, R (2020) A Dialogic Teaching Companion, Routledge, London
2. Bovill, C. (2020) Co-creating Learning and Teaching, Critical Publishing, UK
3. Lofthouse, R., Leat, D. & Towler, C. (2010) Coaching For Teaching and Learning: A Practical Guide For Schools, CfBT Education Trust, UK
4. Sahlberg, P. (2014) in Pollard, A. (2014) Readings For Reflective Teaching in Schools, Bloomsbury, UK
5. Bovill. C. (2020) Co-creating learning and teaching, Critical publishing, UK,
6. Cox, S. in McKie, N. (2021) Persyou Inspirational Leadership podcast, series 5, episode 5
7. Fitzmaurice, A. (2019) Five Trends for Education in 2019 (https://academytoday.co.uk/Article/five-trends-for-education-in-2019)
8. Gallwey, T. (2015) The Inner Game of Tennis, Pan Publishing, UK
9. Roffey, S. (ed.) (2012) Positive Relationships: Evidence Based Practice Across the World, Springer
10. Thayer-Bacon, B (2010) in Bovill, C. (2020) Co-creating Learning and Teaching, Critical Publishing, UK
11. Bovill, C. (2020) Co-creating learning and teaching, Critical publishing, UK,
12. Kukulska-Hulme, A., Bossu, C., Coughlan, T., Ferguson, R., FitzrGerald, E., Gaved, M., Herodotou, C., Rienties, B., Sargent, J., Scanlon, E., Tang, J., Wang, Q., Whitelock D. & Zhang, S. (2021) Innovating Pedagogy 2021, Open University, UK
13. Pollard, A. (2014) Readings for Reflective Teaching in Schools, Bloomsbury, UK
14. Pollard, A. (2014) Readings for Reflective Teaching in Schools, Bloomsbury, UK
15. Deci, E. L. & Ryan, R. M. (2020) Intrinsic and Extrinsic Motivation From a Self-Determination Theory Perspective: Definitions, Theory, Practices, and Future Directions, Contemporary Educational Psychology (www.sciencedirect.com/science/article/pii/S0361476X20300254?via%3Dihub)
16. Coe, R., Rauch, CJ., Kime, S. & Singleton, D. (2020) Great Teaching Toolkit Evidence Review, Cambridge Assessment, UK
17. Levy, D. (2020) The Synchronous vs. Asynchronous Balancing Act, (https://hbsp.harvard.edu/inspiring-minds/the-synchronous-vs-asynchronous-balancing-act?itemFindingMethod=Editorial)
18. Bernard, et al. (2009) A Meta-Analysis of Three Types of Interaction Treatments in Distance Education, Review of Educational Research
19. McAleavy, T. & Gorgen, K. (2020) Overview of Emerging Country Level Response to Providing Educational Continuity Under COVID-19: Best Practice in Pedagogy for Remote Teaching, EdTech Hub and Education Development Trust (https://edtechhub.org/wp-content/uploads/2020/04/research-best-practice-pedagogy-remote-teaching.pdf)
20. Adapted from The Institute of Leadership and Management (2021) (www.institutelm.com/resourceLibrary/the-secrets-to-effective-

teamwork.html?utm_source=Institute%20of%20Leadership%20Management&ut
m_medium=email&utm_campaign=12232226_Onboarding%20Email%204%20-
%20March%202021&dm_i=24KX,7A6G2,W57NOI,TJ4ZQ,1)

21. Adapted from Tocino-Smith, J. (2021) How to Apply Appreciative Inquiry: A
Visual Guide, (https://positivepsychology.com/appreciative-inquiry-process/)

22. Mohr, B. J. & Watkins, J. M. (2002) The Essentials of Appreciative Inquiry: A
Roadmap for Creating Positive Futures. Pegasus Communications, Inc.

23. Montclair State University, US (www.montclair.edu/iapc/)

24 & 25. The National Charity Supporting Philosophy for Children (2021)
(www.sapere.org.uk/about-us.aspx)

26. Stelter, R. (2019) The Art of Dialogue in Coaching, Routledge, UK

27. Alexander, R (2020) A Dialogic Teaching Companion, Routledge, London

28. UCL. (2021) Designing Programmes and Modules with ABC Curriculum
Design (www.ucl.ac.uk/teaching-learning/case-studies/2018/jun/designing-
programmes-and-modules-abc-curriculum-design)

29. Kukulska-Hulme, A., Bossu, C., Coughlan, T., Ferguson, R., FitrzGerald, E.,
Gaved, M., Herodotou, C., Rienties, B., Sargent, J., Scanlon, E., Tang, J., Wang, Q.,
Whitelock D. & Zhang, S. (2021) Innovating Pedagogy 2021, Open University, UK

An Informal Approach

An informal teaching approach involves the teacher standing back, empathising with the learners' goals, acting as a model and resource[1]. This is about the teacher becoming more of a coach and not necessarily being the expert in the room. Independent learning is undertaken in self-managing friendship groups where the content is chosen by the learners. There are no learning objectives and the outcomes of learning are not necessarily known, they unfold. It is often haphazard learning without structured guidance and as such can be challenging, conflicting with our views on professionalism, pedagogical methods and curricular requirements[2].

Unlike more performative, formal approaches, an informal approach is not framed around completion, but collaboration through community. Everyone starts at the same point engaging with tasks that are not differentiated. There is also the potential to use external support from visiting professionals to supplement learning.

Coaching in Informal Teaching

Informal learning is not planned in advance and as such has parallels with the Transformative coaching domain, in which teachers are comfortable with working in 'the space between', where you are not sure of outcomes. In an informal teaching approach, our focus is not external performativity measures and a narrow professional identity but rather the use of internal 'yardsticks' associated to purpose and calling. Egos need to be placed to one side to make decisions that align with deeper inner convictions, such as being true to oneself and your values.

In the same way that effective dialogue is key to Transformative coaching, so it is with an informal teaching approach. Dialogic teaching is a pedagogy of the spoken word that harnesses the power of dialogue, to stimulate and extend students' thinking, learning, knowing and understanding, and to enable them to discuss, reason and argue[3].

Informal learning is highlighted as equally important to formal pedagogy among the ten principles of the UK's Teaching and Learning Research programme[4].

Opportunities need to be developed for students to be exposed to more contemporary and diverse themes[5], allowing students the freedom to connect with wider contexts, not purely focussed on the school setting itself but increasing collaboration with the outside world.

In this teaching approach, school is not a sub-culture of what is going on in the world, there is connection and contextualisation. This aligns with Systemic approaches to coaching that have more emphasis on the context we all operate in[6].

Interdisciplinary teaching

At the University of Warwick, the secondary PGCE team deliver a fascinating lecture on the future of education. As we have explored in the formal approach (in Part 2, Chapter 1), in general education is geared to be disciplinary in nature. We typically study subjects in isolation of each other, to be tested at various stages of our educational life. As teachers we are taught in respect of our subject or phase level: early years, primary and secondary and so on. This is a formal approach to education.

Multidisciplinary teaching and learning encourages students to make meaningful connections between different subject areas, enabling them to develop a range of competencies such as teamwork, problem-solving and communication. Teachers collaboratively plan to facilitate and deliver lessons. This is centred on the co-creation of material outlined in the non-formal approach to teaching.

Interdisciplinary teaching goes a step further, with teachers organising the curriculum around common learning across disciplines. The learning content is self-directed and self-designed by students. They integrate information, methods, tools and perspectives to create 'products', explain phenomena or solve problems. This approach is engaging in that it is relevant to the real world, it breaks down the artificial barriers and hierarchy between subjects and phases and promotes independence and creative thinking from a systemic perspective (see diagram below). Learning can be developed precisely because of the cross-fertilisation of ideas across disciplines.

Interdisciplinary

Multidisciplinary

Disciplinary

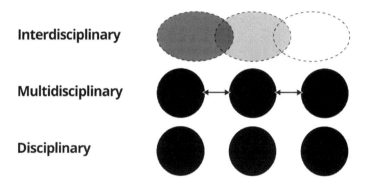

As an example, according to the University of Warwick[7], higher education will increasingly be characterised by being co-created with students, by learning beyond boundaries, greater interdisciplinarity, and by student research. Face-to-face learning, and learning as a social experience, will remain central to the approach.

Phenomenon-based learning

A prime example of interdisciplinary teaching is Phenomenon-based Learning[8] (PhenoBL). PhenoBL is an approach to learning in which students are presented with a phenomenon from the real world. Phenomena are holistic topics such as human, European Union, media and technology, water or energy. Originally from Finland, PhenoBL is now a mandated part of the Finnish National Curriculum Framework alongside subject-specific instruction.

Kirsti Lonka, a professor of educational psychology at Helsinki University states, "When it comes to real life, our brain is not sliced into disciplines [...] we are thinking in a very holistic way. And when you think about the problems in the world – global crises, migration, the economy, the post-truth era – we really haven't given our children the tools to deal with this inter-cultural world."[9]

In PhenoBL there are no lesson objectives or subject steer as found in the other teaching approaches – it is about asking big questions and applying the subjects relevant to that problem. This type of learning shares similarities with systemic pedagogically meaningful methods such as enquiry and problem-based learning. Problem-based learning involves having a class pose a problem to be solved through active learning, while enquiry-based learning involves the use of systematic methods to solve a problem[10]. A key difference, however, is that phenomenon-based learning must have a global context and an interdisciplinary approach[11].

There are five dimensions to a phenomenon-based approach to education centred around 21st century skills[12]:

- holisticity
- authenticity
- contextuality
- problem-based enquiry
- open-ended learning processes

PhenoBL has a lot in common with professional learning communities (PLC), whereby a group of people come together linked by a common interest. As students participate in these informal interdisciplinary ways, they negotiate with others and form and evolve their identities[13]. In terms of how to get these communities up and running, research into PLC implementation in schools in Singapore found a 'tight-loose' approach. That is, tight control from school leadership in terms of setting expectations around PLC initiatives but a loose approach in that departments and teachers decide how they want to implement it[14].

Let us pause and think about the implications for coaching. Firstly, teachers act more like coaches, supporting students through their own chosen learning path. You could argue that there are actually no teachers, only coaches supported by industry experts and knowhow. Teachers (coaches) bring the pedagogy not necessarily the expertise. Secondly, in Finland we have an example of an education system with no school inspections, no lesson observations and few external exams[15].

Consider how this frees teachers to develop their own areas of interest and their ability to cross pollinate with other teachers and professionals across sectors. This is emblematic of the Transformative coaching domain in that structures and boundaries are not thought of as important, it is the collaboration through networking.

Of course, this way of teaching raises questions around how to go about planning and preparing for such an approach. In the same way that we crave the safety of models in coaching, so too as teachers we look to have at least some curricula framework from which to build on, as is found in formal education.

Informal teaching in practice

What does the informal approach look like? At the Evangelical School Berlin Centre (ESBC) in Germany there are no timetables, no traditional lessons and no grades awarded until students turn 15 years of age. The students themselves decide which subjects they want to study – progressing beyond the traditional student-voice school projects – developing self-motivation and an ability to deal with change and ambiguity.

The ESBC headteacher is trying to do nothing less than 'reinvent what a school is'. 'The mission of a progressive school should be to prepare young people to cope with change, or better still, to make them look forward to change. In the 21st century, schools should see it as their job to develop strong personalities.'[16]

The Agora School in Roermond, The Netherlands, also espouses an unconventional educational approach. There are no year groups and assessments. Students self-manage with the freedom to design and explore projects accompanied by specialist teacher coaches. The rationale for this approach is that traditional education does not prepare students for the skills demanded of them in the wider world.

'The children at Agora are different, like us adults they have the world's information in their pocket, but crucially, they have the wherewithal to make sense of it, synthesise and use it as and when they need it. And chief among their soft skills is a sense of confidence in their abilities to tackle problems and communicate with adults and each other.'[17]

Interestingly, the teacher acts as a coach in that he or she frames learning and brings in specialists to provide key real-world knowledge, an approach that requires expert generalists with specialist skills able to work across age groups and disciplines. This is about understanding the context in which you work (not simply in the classroom).

Vikram Mansharamani from Harvard University refers to how a way of thinking rather than specific skills will equip people for the future: 'Generalists with breadth of perspective and the ability to connect the proverbial dots (the domain of generalists) is likely to be as important as depth of expertise and the ability to generate dots (the domain of specialists).'[18]

A friction then exists, a clash in ideologies between a formal and informal outlook. The ESBC and Agora schools demonstrate the informal teaching approach, in contrast to formal education based around a performative culture in which it could be argued that results are valued over people.

Interestingly, a survey of over 10,000 members of an education union in the UK concluded that the vast majority of school staff supported working with students 'in a way that is nimble and unconstrained by curriculum diktat, with active and creative elements forming a strong part of that approach.'[19]

82% of those surveyed believed that flexibility was key, evidence perhaps of an appetite in the UK education system to delve further into non-formal and informal approaches.

Dave Strudwick, Principal of the REAL School, Budapest talks about creativity being an essential part of creating informal learning: 'Three processes – coaching, choreography and conducting – are all important at different times. You need to give space and confidence for people to experiment.'[20]

The creative teacher will incorporate coaching skills and approaches and be[21]:

- at ease in ambiguity and complexity
- synthesising elements of your role rather than operating in isolation
- not afraid of being wrong
- engaging high levels of questioning and listening throughout all interactions

Critical Instructional Design

A couple of years ago I attended a fascinating workshop on critical instructional design led by Sean Michael Morris, Senior Instructor of Learning Design and Technology in the School of Education and Human Development at the University of Colorado, Denver. 'The critical instructional design approach prioritizes collaboration, participation, social justice, learner agency, emergence, narrative, and relationships of nurture between students, and between teachers and students.'[22]

Morris opened the workshop by talking us through the reasons why he doesn't use traditional assessments, including assessment rubrics or learning objectives and intentions. You could feel the scepticism in the room! His reasoning was that learner contributions are meaningful to the courses he teaches, there are no right answers to the questions he is bound to ask. Essentially, he could spend time building assessments for the courses he teaches, but that would require a sense that learners would accomplish what he wants them to learn.

One of the key tenets of critical instructional design is that of emergence, that outcomes are determined by the learning process itself. There is a caveat here, in that Morris predominately teaches at university level, with learners capable of driving this emergent learning. There are great parallels with the Transformative coaching domain, in that we are free to explore where the dialogue takes us. This is not prescribed coaching.

Summary

In the informal approach, the teacher is now the coach. Their role is not to teach and plan content but to support learning through utilising all coaching domains. The Transformative domain is key through developing effective dialogue, working in the 'space between' to extend learning and understanding.

- Learning content is chosen by the students
- No learning objectives and learning outcomes are not necessarily known
- Teacher stands back and acts as a coach creating the best environment for learning
- Understanding is demonstrated in groups as well as individuals

References

1. Musical Futures (2020) (www.musicalfutures.org/who-we-are)
2. Green, L. (2008) Music, Informal Learning and The School, Ashgate Publishing, UK
3. Alexander, R. (2020) A Dialogic Teaching Companion, Routledge, London
4. Pollard, A. (2018) Reflective Teaching in Schools, Bloomsbury Academic, UK
5. Swanwick, K. (1988) Music, Mind, and Education, Routledge, London, UK
6. Wright, A., McLean Walsh, M. & Tennyson, S. (2019) Systemic Coaching Supervision: Responding to the Complex Challenges of Our Time, Philosophy of Coaching: An International Journal, Vol.4, No.1, May 2019
7. The University of Warwick. (2018) (https://warwick.ac.uk/about/strategy/education/)
8. Silander, P (2019) Phenomenon Based Learning, (www.phenomenaleducation.info/phenomenon-based-learning.html)
9. Jezard, A. (2017) Is This Finnish School the Perfect Design? (www.weforum.org/agenda/2017/10/why-finland-is-tearing-down-walls-in-schools/)
10. Drew, C. (2020) What is Finland's Phenomenon-based Learning Approach? (www.teachermagazine.com/au_en/articles/what-is-finlands-phenomenon-based-learning-approach)
11. Valamis. (2019) What is phenomenon-based learning? (www.valamis.com/hub/phenomenon-based-learning)
12. Symeonidis, V. & Schwarz, J. F. (2016) Phenomenon-based Teaching and Learning Through the Pedagogical Lenses of Phenomenology: The Recent Curriculum Reform in Finland. Forum Oświatowe
13. Kukulska-Hulme, A., Bossu, C., Coughlan, T., Ferguson, R., FitrzGerald, E., Gaved, M., Herodotou, C., Rienties, B., Sargent, J., Scanlon, E., Tang, J., Wang, Q., Whitelock D. & Zhang, S. (2021) Innovating Pedagogy 2021, Open University, UK
14. Ho, J., Ong, M. & Tan, L. (2019) Leadership of Professional Learning Communities in Singaporean Schools in Educational Management Administration and Leadership Journal, Vol.48 No.4, July 2020, BELMAS, UK
15. Crehan, L. (2016) Clever Lands, Unbound, London, UK
16. Oltermann, P. (2016) No Grades, No Timetable: Berlin School Turns Teaching Upside Down (www.theguardian.com/world/2016/jul/01/no-grades-no-timetable-berlin-school-turns-teaching-upside-down)
17. Webb, A (2019) Meet the School With No Classes, No Classrooms and No Curriculum (https://medium.com/pi-top/meet-the-school-with-no-classes-no-classrooms-and-no-curriculum-7cc7be517cef)
18. Mansharamani, V. (2020) No Specific Skill Will Get You Ahead in the Future, (www-cnbc-com.cdn.ampproject.org/c/s/www.cnbc.com/amp/2020/06/15/harvard-yale-researcher-future-success-is-not-a-specific-skill-its-a-type-of-thinking.html)
19. Weale, S. (2021) Covid: Teachers Reject Catchup Options of Extended School Day and Shorter Holidays

(www.theguardian.com/education/2021/apr/07/teachers-reject-covid-catchup-options-of-extended-school-day-and-shorter-holidays)
20. Strudwick, D. in McKie, N. (2021) Persyou Inspiring Leadership podcast, series 4, episode 12
21. Adapted from West-Burnham, J. (1997) Managing Quality in Schools, Pearson Education, UK
22. Morris, SM. (2017) A Call for Critical Instructional Design
(www.seanmichaelmorris.com/a-call-for-critical-instructional-design/)

Part Two: Chapter 4

Blending the Three Approaches in Your Setting

To enact a coaching way of teaching we need a blended application of all three approaches: formal, non-formal and informal.

Firstly, we can focus on the individual teacher engaging with the three approaches across their own practice in a series of lessons or over a longer period of time. This is a progression from teacher to facilitator to coach. What might this look like?

In a formal approach the **teacher** will:

- be contracting to set behaviour expectations
- be planning sequenced lessons including objectives and outcomes and engaging students through questioning, assessment and feedback
- teaching will be directive and knowledge-based around curriculum, exams and tests have a reliance on benchmarking of standards in relation to appraisals and observations
- timetable lessons around phases, age and subjects

In a non-formal approach the **facilitator** will:

- co-create content with the students
- display fundamental coaching skills such as active listening, open questioning as well as recognising energy blocks such a limiting beliefs and assumptions that prevent learning taking place

- focus on the student, developing self-management with the facilitator showing sensitivity to student's needs
- harness group coaching techniques as the learning environment becomes more fluid such as action learning sets and team coaching methodology
- still scaffold learning at times with students developing agency

In an informal approach the **coach** will:

- stand back and become less of a teacher and more of a coach
- support learning rather than being the expert at all times; outcomes are determined by the learning process itself
- allow the breakdown of hierarchy and encourage effective dialogue at the heart of interactions
- allow students to choose content, across a range of subjects and phases
- remove timetabling and place the onus on the development of teams and shared learning

In practice, in the classroom, the boundaries between formal and informal learning are not always clear and any lesson may include elements of each. Embrace the ambiguity of there not being only one way[1].

In a wider sense it is possible to implement a blend of the three approaches across year groups, phases and age groups. Vertical tutoring and grouping across age ranges are the perfect environment for this to happen. The key element here is to have an awareness of different pedagogical approaches and plan (or not!) accordingly.

It is possible to look wider still, with a nod to the coaching union outlined in Part 1. Schools can connect regionally, nationally and internationally to develop non-formal and informal pedagogy. This is where we begin to move beyond formal exam-focussed education to a people-focussed model and to a coaching way of teaching.

In the same way that we shift responsibility from the teacher to the student we must also trust the teaching profession to drive and develop the sector. We are very good at giving students more autonomy but also need to ensure we do that with educational professionals.

Like the coaching unions, we need to craft time and space to enable teachers to collaborate and coach each other across the sector, not in isolation. Using systemic coaching techniques such as action learning sets to connect (including across schools) can be invaluable in developing effective transformational dialogue.

References

1. Hallam, S., Andrea, C. & Hilary, M. (2017), Classroom Resources
for Informal Music Learning at Key Stage 3, Musical Futures, Paul Hamlyn
Foundation Special project,
(file:///C:/Users/u4050008/Downloads/Informal%20Learning%20Model%20R
esource.pdf)

Part Three

A Coaching Way of Leading

In this section we will explore the idea that contemporary leadership practice aligns with the skills and approaches of effective coaching. I'd like you to take away a fresh perspective on how to deploy coaching in your leadership practice.

You will notice an overlap with the skills and approaches you need to be an effective coach, utilising the three coaching domains outlined in Part 1 as well as the practices discussed in Part 2.

This section is applicable for anyone who has leadership responsibilities and is aspiring to lead in their context. It is also just as relevant to anyone in education looking to develop their role.

A coaching leadership style has the potential to improve performance, support greater staff autonomy and teamwork and encourage confidence and ambition. This is achieved through the development of each of the following, explored in the chapters of Part 3:

- self-awareness
- relationships
- agility

When we become self-aware, we can then develop new and deeper relationships. This allows us to empower people and enable learning. When we build on this with the ability to be agile, we are able to deal with change and complexity. When fused with the three coaching domains, this is the coaching way of leading, as illustrated in the diagram overleaf:

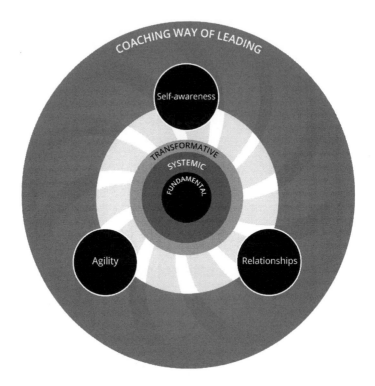

In coaching school leaders and producing my Persyou podcast series *Inspiring Leadership* I have had the opportunity to talk to world-class leaders and leadership experts from across the global education sector and beyond. I draw upon these experiences throughout this chapter to help illustrate points.

You will see a podcast icon next to some quotations throughout Part 3 and I invite you to delve into these insightful conversations in full to supplement your own learning. All *Inspiring Leadership* podcasts are available to listen to on the Persyou website (www.persyou.com) and on all the usual podcast platforms.

Part Three: Chapter 1

Self-awareness

I'd like you to read the following and identify how many Fs you count:

FINISHED FILES ARE THE RE-
SULT OF MANY YEARS OF SCIENTIF-
IC STUDY COMBINED WITH THE
EXPERIENCE OF MANY YEARS.

This is an exercise from Clive Woodward's book *Winning*[1], in which he outlines the England rugby team's journey to a Rugby World Cup win in 2003. Commonly people will see three Fs, although there are actually six, most missing the Fs in the three instances of 'OF'. The exercise was one of my staple ice-breakers when I was a school leader, demonstrating to staff how aware we actually are in our day-to-day lives. If we are missing half of what is in front of us then there is plenty for us to become aware of!

I believe self-awareness is the foundation for effective leadership. This includes understanding who you are, what you can do, what you can't do, where your values come from and where you need improvement[2]. Being more aware is also about being in tune with your thoughts, feelings and actions and in relation to other people and the environment around you[3]. It offers a new way to consider events, people and processes, enabling educational leaders to better understand complex situations that arise in their setting[4].

As leaders we tend to be very good at being self-conscious: 'do people think I'm up to the job?' Or, 'are people judging my ability?' for example. This is ego thinking and can weigh heavily. In self-consciousness the focus is purely on the self, whilst in self-awareness the focus shifts to awareness[5]. When this happens, you are no longer concerned with the opinion and judgements of other people, rather you are focussed on being aware of what is unfolding before you. This draws on the Systemic coaching domain, in terms of having an awareness of the patterns at play in the systems in which you belong.

Self-awareness also links to the Transformative domain in relation to developing your coaching philosophy and way of being, through connection, confidence, courage and continuing. When coaching leaders, I find that once people are aware of the way they operate – tendencies, bias and potential blind spots, for example – other things fall into place across all aspects of their lives.

Self-awareness is always with us but our way of thinking and the day-to-day nuts and bolts of our working (and non-working) lives often obscure it. In Part 1, we explored this as part of the Transformative domain, in relation to working in the 'space between' and also grounding through the centre, widen and listen techniques, as well as using nature to become more present and aware.

This is why your coaching evolution is key. As a leader, your work in the Transformative coaching domain offers you a path towards being better at seeing, accepting and integrating the different elements of yourself, and therefore impacting interactions with others.

There are six key tenets to creating self-awareness for a coaching way of leading:

1. Multi-source feedback
2. Systemic awareness
3. Energy leadership
4. Strengths and stretch
5. Identity
6. Rest

Multi-source Feedback

There are a number of diagnostic tools available to assess how you turn up both at work and at home, covering aspects such as emotions, relationships, thinking and execution[6]. I use these when coaching education leaders and they can be beneficial as a tangible, objective assessment, not influenced by other parties and therefore not a personal judgment. Such tools can be an eye-opening way of igniting leadership development but only when used as a starting point, not as labelling – while developing awareness it is key to keep an open mind.

I find the best assessments are attitudinal in nature, taking a snapshot of how people are operating at a particular time and place. There has been a lot of discussion in recent years about looking deeply inside to find your true self, but we have to be flexible when making judgements on our self. Be wary of your energy blocks here, specifically limiting beliefs and deep-seated gremlins! Instead of thinking of yourself in set ways, think of yourself as a complex array of emotions, dispositions, desires and traits that often pull you in different and contradictory ways[7].

Gathering multi-source feedback (i.e.., from various rather than just one source) is also a beneficial way of developmental appraisal, raising awareness of how you are operating, and is a form of appraisal commonly associated with senior leaders. I find that this 360-degree approach is potentially a way of making the appraisal process less subjective.

Multi-source feedback[8] and 360-degree appraisal concepts are based on the view that feedback from different sources allows for more balance and objectivity than does the single view of, for example, a line manager.

When administrating leadership assessment, I find it beneficial to refer to the school stakeholders outlined in the Systemic domain in Part 1. Aim to get at least one person from each of the stakeholder groups which includes non-teaching staff and community as well as teaching staff.

Systemic Awareness

Educational leaders can feel that they are, of necessity, right in the middle of the complexity (and perhaps chaos) of their role. Looking at the world through such a lens can encourage us to watch out for patterns of conversation, to recognise how meaning spreads quickly through social networks[9].

We therefore require a systemic mindset to see the whole picture. This is about addressing all of the systems at play within an organisation as well as the stakeholders involved in the multi-source feedback.

You can begin to develop systemic awareness by reflecting on[10]:

- How would you describe the system or context to which you belong?
- How aware are you of the interactions and interdependences of the various parts of your system?
- How do these interactions influence your life?
- What parts of your system needs attention?

As a leader with a systemic mindset you will look beyond individual behaviour when seeking to understand events.

You will need to be visible and 'on the ground' looking to understand the social and power dynamics at play.

Energy Leadership

I'd like to refer once again to the idea of energy. As mentioned in the Fundamental domain in Part 1, catabolic and anabolic energy refers to the destructive and constructive energy at play within an individual or organisation. In terms of developing self-awareness, it can be worth considering whether you are a catabolic or anabolic leader.

The catabolic leader manages by control, gives information without justification, works in crisis mode, emotionally disconnects, focusses on problems and takes advantage of staff.

The anabolic leader sees only opportunities. They encourage others to develop, shares information, gets feedback and buy in and is future focussed[11].

But few individuals display such binary energy, they are not entirely one or the other. If we look in more detail, we can begin to understand progressive energy levels. In the lowest form of catabolic energy we feel victims in life and engage in conflict. I am sure that we recognise times when both ourselves and others have been resonating at these levels.

As a leader, I actually welcome anger occasionally from teams as this shows that people are at least engaged! When people are disengaged you have a problem, so it is the time spent at these lower energy levels that is key. Once we recognise that we are being victims (and have usually vented our frustrations) then it is about taking the responsibility to forgive and move forward through compassion and reconciliation into more growth-orientated anabolic energy.

As a leader you can support this by being visible and incorporating your coaching domains to more fully understand how people feel.

The highest anabolic energy levels are concerned with wisdom, joy and non-judgment. In the same way, in the Transformative coaching domain we recognise the lack of systems and structure, so we see no limitations in this energy, only opportunities. When we have such awareness and clarity, we can take ourselves outside of a situation to observe and see things for what they are. At this stage we are allowing the energy to flow through everything we do, we are energised and fully aware.

> **Tip:**
>
> When cultivating your own self-awareness look to the energy blocks (GAILS) outlined in the Fundamental coaching domain. What is it that is holding you back and preventing you from resonating in the higher anabolic levels? As a leader you will recognise the energy levels in the people you work with.
>
> Use your coaching skills to challenge thinking, help break through the blocks and move forward whether in formal meetings or more informal interactions.

Leadership Wheel

If you do not have access or the resource to engage with a coaching diagnostic tool then another way of developing your self-awareness can be through using a leadership wheel, as illustrated in the diagram opposite[12].

Simply rank your current perceived effectiveness of the different elements around the wheel and rank yourself from one (not at all happy) to ten (extremely happy). Once you have done this for each element you can then join the dots to present an overall picture of your current leadership practice and approach.

Ask yourself what the wheel is telling you: you can see areas that you are currently excelling in and set targets and strategies based on these findings. The elements are a guide and are open to change to fit your specific context.

Tip:

I have found this also works well as part of a team mapping exercise to identify areas for improvement for your team. In this case, as a leader you can utilise your facilitation skills (as outlined in the group and team coaching sections in the Systemic domain) to bring out the best reflections in others.

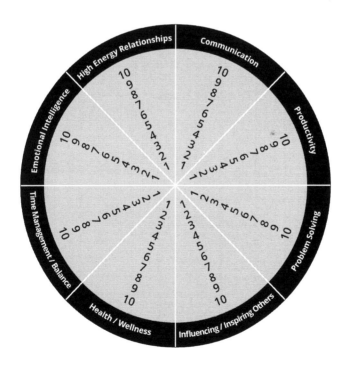

Strengths and Stretch:
Using your strengths to meet the demands of your role

Once you have an increased awareness of the areas that enthuse you, and your strengths, you can begin to leverage these to support your leadership development. Strengths can be defined as: 'underlying qualities that energise us, and we are great at (or have the potential to become great at)'[13]. This starts with the premise that as human beings we are not problems waiting to be solved but potential waiting to unfold[14]. I love this anabolic thinking!

You can optimise your strengths in the following ways[15]:

- **Experience** new learning on and off the job
  - o This could include areas that you are currently working in or seeking opportunities outside of your role where you can utilise your strengths. This could also include supporting others to develop their expertise in areas that enthuse you.
- **Engage** other to support and coach you
  - o This is about connecting as a leader, putting your ego to one side and knowing who to go to for the type of support that you need.
- **Educate** yourself to develop your knowledge and skills
  - o This could be through qualifications, engagement in literature or listening to leadership and education-related podcasts for example.

Brian Cooklin, Managing Director at international school group Nord Anglia Education, illustrates these points and believes that those striving for high performance leadership need to ensure they themselves continue to learn: 'Meeting speakers, reading different authors, research articles, it's all CPD. I'm always looking to challenge my ideas. I make myself available to coach or mentor others. What people forget when they're coaching is that you are learning at the same time.'

Mandy Coalter, Founder of Talent Architects also sees leadership training as integral to success of an organisation: 'We've got to get over this hurdle of seeing leadership training as a luxury. It isn't. If people don't lead well that has all sorts of positive implications.'

Stretch

The most effective leaders positively challenge and stretch themselves and the teams around them, strengthening their own learning, whilst also pushing the boundaries of possibility. To stretch yourself in a positive way, the first step is to understand which activities are challenging you.

It is then possible to stretch those areas which naturally provide growth and motivation rather than concentrate on your perceived areas of weakness. We tend to get what we focus on – so when we focus on what we *can* do, this helps eliminate the fear and anxiety of not being able to do something.

When coaching leaders in education I have found it helpful to incorporate the 'stretch zone model'[16] which can be an effective way of igniting a coaching dialogue.

This model outlines three zones:

- comfort
- stretch
- panic

The aim is to understand more about what makes you operate in each zone, with an idea of moving beyond your comfort zone into your stretch zone, without progressing into your panic zone. Positive stretch involves challenging people in their areas of strengths to enable them to learn and grow. For example, someone who has a skill for curriculum planning being invited to feed into whole school development planning. Negative stretch is where the focus is in an area of weakness where they are not supported[17] and commonly results in entering the panic zone. An example of this would be starting a new school without an adequate induction and being expected to know all of the procedures and systems at play.

The key here is to identify your point of difference in terms of the unique strengths you bring to your role. Once identified, then look to 'strengthen your strengths'. Once you become aware of your skills, knowledge, strengths and energisers, look to see where these are aligned with your schools or institutions mission and goals. If these elements are aligned, then you can know that you are working in a place that is suitable for you and one in which you can be effective in your role and grow. How many times in an appraisal or performance management conversation have you been told to focus on weaknesses? How about if you were told to focus on one or two of your strengths to make these world class for example?

If you discover your strengths are not aligned to your setting, then you may find that there are not opportunities for you to showcase and engage in work that energises you which can lead to frustration and ultimately an exit.

Leader Identity

Once you become more self-aware and have a solid grasp of your strengths you can begin to develop your leadership identity. One's leadership identity can be described as: 'working self-concept that includes leadership schemas, leadership experience and future representations of oneself as a leader.'[18]

This includes the dynamic process and interaction between the individual and social environment of which you are part[19].

Leadership identity can be described in three stages[20]:

- under-developed
- forming
- well developed

The **under-developed** leader does not see themselves as a leader and they identify with other professional identities (e.g., I am a teacher); their self-identity as a leader is not internalised.

The **forming** leader does begin to see themselves as a leader however their identity is still developing. They begin to experiment with different leadership approaches to craft their leader identity (e.g., I am a teacher and I know I am becoming a leader). They may have some insecurities about whether they are capable of taking the step into leadership, questioning if other people believe that they know what they are doing.

The **well-developed** leader begins to internalise their leader identity as a part of who they are (e.g., I am a leader and a teacher). Leadership is who they are as a person, it is their 'way of being'. In the same way as coaching in the Transformative domain, there is an underlying feeling of mastery in your leadership that gives significance and value to your work.

I find that a job title has little to do with one's leadership identity. Just because someone is a headteacher doesn't necessarily equate to a well-developed leadership identity. Key for me is, does the headteacher recognise their own leadership identity, are they open enough to embrace it and look to develop their leadership? In terms of coaching for leadership development, that I can work with.

When speaking to UK National Boxing Champion Sedem Ama[21] she put her success down to the fact that she is coachable, able to pick up skills in a short period of time and perform well too. Being coachable and open to development is more important than a current stage of leadership identity.

I hear a lot of the leaders who I coach talk about wanting to be 'authentic'. In the same way as it can be limiting to define who you are based solely on the labels gained via leadership assessments, so too can we constrict our view of what makes us 'authentic'.

Social context has a bearing on the way people 'turn up'. Leaders may be authentic in terms of the identity they have in their role – it may demand certain traits that are different to the identity of the person outside of a work setting. Is it possible to be truly authentic as a leader in all interactions?

Setting goals and targets can be positive but can also limit opportunities to truly develop ourselves. Be adaptive when seeking authenticity, circumstances change and your ability to be agile is key (see Part 3, Chapter 3).

How can coaching support leadership identity?

Several studies show that coaching has a positive impact on a leader's personality and identity alleviating[22]:

- neuroticism
- anxiety and fears
- impostor tendencies
- emotional volatility

Coaching can help leaders develop their identity at all stages by supporting transitions across identity boundaries. I find that coaching is often called upon only once there is an issue with leadership performance.

Example:

A few years ago I was asked by a US college to 'coach' a member of staff who had already been through a disciplinary panel and was found guilty of bullying other members of their team after a promotion. The member of staff had been warned on a number of occasions, with minimal support provided. Firstly, I put it to the college that this was not a 'coaching' assignment, this was more disciplinary in nature. Secondly, I was curious as to why the support was being put in now rather than before the issues arose. Coaching should be utilised before this point is reached, during and after transitions of any kind, not simply when things are going wrong.

Any under-developed leader will benefit from coaching as they navigate their way into the forming leader stage. How often do we see an excellent classroom teacher promoted to a leadership position without sufficient support? The same is true of middle leaders in schools who are catapulted into senior roles without the opportunity to truly form their leadership identity. This is putting people into the 'panic zone' without a supported stretch.

Individual mapping, found in the Systemic domain, can have real impact in supporting people as they are promoted. It enables them to see themselves within the system in which they belong, aware of the narratives at play and the context as they step into their next role.

Identity in groups and teams

Awareness of identity is also key in terms of the groups and teams of which we are a part. As previously outlined in the Systemic domain (in Part 1), groups are defined as where people have a shared interest but no collective responsibility to deliver results, whereas teams have collective purpose and objective which all members are jointly responsible for fulfilling[23].

If people are socially connected then they are more like a group. You can have a group of people who are loosely connected socially but never make it into a great team because they lack identity. I have seen this in the international education 'bubble' where people are living and working closely together and the lines can get blurred between professional and personal. People are socially connected in work.

If people are relationally connected then they are more like a team. This has to have identity at the heart of it.

Ask your team the following to get an idea of your collective identity[24]:

- Why are you working together?
- What are your shared values, symbols, rituals, language and guiding principles?

Once you have answered these questions and have a collective understanding, you can develop your team (see Part 3, Chapter 2).

Rest: What's your Speed Bump?

The 2021 International School Teacher Wellbeing report[25] found that many international schoolteachers felt overwhelmed, with a high level of work-related stress during the COVID pandemic.

While this is perhaps unsurprising, for most this stress was caused specifically by:

- increased workload
- the demands of implementing online and blended learning models
- the blurring of boundaries between home and work
- the pressure of demands and expectations placed on teachers by school leaders and parents

Most teachers have implemented coping strategies but for some these strategies have had a limited impact on their overall wellbeing[26].

Although not a substitute for therapy, a research report into the Impact of Leadership Coaching in Schools[27] found coaching to have a positive impact on headteachers' self-belief and confidence, and coaching helped them to place greater priority on their physical health. Coaching also helped to address the feelings of isolation commonly felt by headteachers.

Self-awareness is also about knowing when to keep going and when to rest, which I refer to as encountering a speed bump in your hectic schedule. Self-care and putting yourself first as a leader shouldn't be neglected, but often is in an education setting. I would go so far as to say this is one of the most common issues to crop up in leadership coaching conversations.

Claudia Hammond[28] outlines the top ten activities which people find the most restful based on the largest global study into rest ever taken. Take a look at the activities below and see which resonate with you.

- Reading
- Spending time in nature
- Spending time alone
- Listening to music
- Doing nothing in particular
- A good walk
- A hot bath
- Daydreaming
- Watching television
- Practising mindfulness

Tip:

Although paradoxical, some people need to be active or undertake exercise to be able to rest. Others are the complete opposite; they can best rest by reading all day, for example. Take the time to reflect upon how often you 'actively' engage in rest and whether that method is most suitable for you.

Get ploughing

Recent research[29] has centred on the experiences of aspiring school principals receiving coaching as part of a leadership development programme. The research found that these leaders enjoyed having time to reflect, felt safe to explore themes, focussed on what's important for them as well as experiencing positive emotions.

When I was a Vice Principal of a school in the UK, the Head (my line manager) used to take Thursday mornings to work away from the school. It happened to coincide with all kinds of issues every week and every Thursday was like an in-tray exercise for me! At the time this was frustrating but looking back I can now understand that there needs to be time away from the chalkface.

When you find yourself with too much on your plate have the self-awareness to arrange a 'ploughing day'. A ploughing day is a ringfenced day when you can behave like a farmer: get up early, get things done and clear your desk as far as possible[30].

Leaders can be their own worst enemy – in my coaching work I often hear the guilt that leaders feel, simply for putting themselves first to allow time to get their own job done. It is crucial to create space to be able to do your job effectively. As a school leader, this may mean that an 'open door' policy is not achievable all the time. This is fine. I invite you to get ploughing!

Summary

Self-awareness is the first step to cultivating a coaching way of leading. You can begin to develop this area through:

- Multi-source feedback appraisals and informal conversations can provide valuable information of how you work.
- Systemic awareness by becoming more in tune with the people you work with and the context in which you work.
- Notice what kind of energy you bring to your leadership, is this growth orientated and forward thinking?
- Recognise where you currently reside in relation to developing your leadership identity. Identify your strengths and identify how you will stretch these to learn and grow in your role.
- Ensure you prioritise rest and time to get things done. It is ok to put yourself first and 'get ploughing'.

References

1. Woodward, C. (2004) Winning, Hodder and Stoughton, UK
2. Stein Jr, A. (2019) Raise Your Game, Center Street, US
3. Widdowson, L. & Barbour, P. (2021) Building Top Performing Teams, KoganPage, UK
4. Shaked, H. & Schechter, C. (2020) Systemic Thinking Leadership: New Explorations For School Improvement in Management in Education. Vol.34, No.3, July 2020
5. Osho, (2012) Learning to Silence the Mind, Osho International Foundation, New York
6. Strengthscope (2017) Energising Peak Performance and Engagement, Strengths Partnership Ltd, UK
7. Puett, M. & Gross-Leh, C. (2016) The Path, Penguin Books, UK
8. Kettley, P. (1997) in Bratton, J. & Gold, J. (2007 4th Ed), Human Resource Management, Theory and Practice, Palgrave Macmillan, US
9. Lawrence, P. (2021) Group Coaching, A Powerful Intervention, White Paper, Centre for Coaching in Organisations, Australia
10. Widdowson, L. & Barbour, P. (2021) Building Top Performing Teams, KoganPage, UK
11. Schneider, B. (2008) Energy Leadership, Wiley and Sons, US
12. iPEC (2013), Coaching Training Manual, US
13. Strengthscope (2017) Energising Peak Performance and Engagement, Strengths Partnership Ltd, UK
14. LaLoux, F. (2014) Reinventing Organisations, Nelson Parker, US
15 & 16 & 17. Strengthscope (2017) Energising peak performance and engagement, Strengths Partnership Ltd, UK
18. Epitropaki, et al (2017) in Skinner, S. (2020) Towards a Theory of Leader Identity Formation and Its Application to Executive Coaching, Philosophy of Coaching: An International Journal, Vol. 5, No.1, May 2020
19. Stelter, R. (2019) The Art of Dialogue in Coaching, Routledge, UK
20. Skinner, S. (2020) Towards a Theory of Leader Identity Formation and Its Application to Executive Coaching, Philosophy of Coaching: An International Journal, Vol. 5 No.1, May 2020
21. Sedem, A.. in McKie, N. (2021) Persyou Inspiring Leadership podcast, series 5, episode 3
22. De Haan, E. (2021) Coaching Today, April 2021
23. Hawkins, P. & Turner, E. (2020) System Coaching, Routledge, UK
24. Grange, P. & Levett, R. (2021) (https://eightypercentmental.com/2021/03/01/2-02-how-do-we-get-team-culture-right/amp/)
24 & 25. Kelly, H. (2021) International School Teacher Wellbeing During the COVID-19 Pandemic, The 2021 Report, The Positive Principal

26. Lofthouse, R. & Whiteside, R. (2020) Sustaining a Vital Profession; A Research Report Into the Impact of Leadership Coaching in School, CollectivED at Leeds Beckett University

27. Hammond, C. (2019) The Art of Rest, Cannongate Books, UK

28. Van Nieuwerburgh, C., Barr, M., Munro, C., Noon, H. & Arifin, D. (2020) Experiences of Aspiring School Principals Receiving Coaching as Part of a Leadership Development Programme, International Journal of Mentoring and Coaching in Education, Vol.9 No.3

29. Jetha, S. (2019) The Smarts, Penguin, UK

Part Three: Chapter 2

Relationships

'Schools are all about people. As a founding Head I have got to make sure that the values that make a school unique are truly embedded through the people of the school' says Michelle Scott, founding Head of Downe House, Muscat in Oman.

To get anything done you need to have relationships. Whether working as a professional musician, teaching, leading schools in different countries, training teachers or coaching leaders in education and beyond, the one constant in my career has been working with people.

When people feel listened to, feel their opinion matters, believe that you want them involved and are acknowledged by you then they will feel like they are in partnership with you[1]. Outstanding leaders perceive relationships as the route to performance. They give huge amounts of their time and focus to people and the climate of the organisation2. When there are issues and challenges it is the power of relationships with a plurality of people that ensures opportunities for reflection, success and support[3].

A coaching way of leading necessitates developing a wide network of relationships, working beyond institution boundaries and potentially spending time outside of your traditional place of work when possible to enable learning. This relates to a coaching culture and union; school leaders increasingly need to develop relationships, networks and partnerships with other school leaders as part of their role.

This area of collaboration is crucial to facilitate change in the larger systems of which they are a part, in a meaningful way[4].

There are seven aspects to relationship building for a coaching way of leading, explored in this chapter:

1. Communication
2. Trust and respect
3. Developing relationships through dialogue
4. Building teams
5. Collaboration
6. Developing psychological safety
7. High value teams

Communication

In schools, social relationships are fundamental and the most significant factor in relationship building. The behaviour of leaders will be a key determinant in creating a conducive environment[5]. As outlined in Part 3, Chapter 1, developing an awareness of how you yourself operate will support your relationship with yourself, so enhancing the quality of relationships with others.

The Fundamental coaching skills such as listening, acknowledging and empathising are particularly relevant here to support and promote engagement. As a leader you also want to ensure you are consistently clarifying to make sure you understand issues and challenges. If a member of staff tells you that that the workload is 'too much', you must understand what they mean by 'too much'.

Once you have effective communication in place you can then begin to develop relationships. Good communication allows you to challenge the people you work with and your teams in an effective way – not overwhelming but strengthening and uplifting.

Effective leadership communication requires emotional intelligence which can be described as[6]:

- developing self-awareness
- self-management
- social awareness
- social skills

Using emotional intelligence in your communication allows you to build relationships across your school community: with your board, staff, parents, students as well as with the local community and fellow schools. It also requires you to be engaging in dialogue with people across your setting.

'If people see you as having honesty, integrity, fairness, then when you have those tough calls, to make things better, then you can still do that,' says Jason McBride, Head of United World College, Thailand. In the current context of blended or virtual learning and online meetings, 'building that relationship bank is tough to do' but being visible as a leader is essential: 'If you don't plan it, it won't happen.'

Good communications with stakeholders are non-negotiable when it comes to leadership. In the COVID pandemic, although face-to-face opportunities became logistically more difficult for many of us, it seems that paradoxically, communication may have improved.

'I've seen a lot of schools up their game in terms of their relationships with parents," says Rt Hon Lord Jim Knight, Chief Education Advisor at TES Global. 'Parents have become closer to being collaborators in learning. Parents have always cared about learning but the lead role has been with the teacher, that's become blurred and communication has been improved.'

There is plenty of evidence that encouraging parents to be more involved in the education of their children leads to better pupil outcomes.

'We're always talking to and coaching parents on why we do things this way, to encourage that faith and build that trusting culture," says Jason McBride. 'Communication is key about what high performance looks like.'

Craig Considine, CEO of Tanglin Trust School in Singapore, concurs in terms of increased communication. During the restrictions and school closures caused by the pandemic, he held regular meetings with small groups of parents from each year group at the school. 'For me, it's the barometer, it gives me understanding of what's going on. It allows me to ask the right questions of my leaders. You could say we're over-communicating, but I think in the world at the moment that's a pretty good way to go.'

As leaders we need to ensure that we have open communication across our places of work. In education, it sometimes feels like we work in our own worlds, going down a subject specialisation route that can in fact hinder communication and the sharing of best practice or development. I remember working in an international 'through' school in China where primary and secondary phases simply didn't collaborate or link effectively.

I also notice this in teacher training. The PGCE international course I lead has been developed with shared expertise from all age phases which has really supported the learning of teaching. Themes such as behaviour and planning are relevant to all teachers, whereas in typical UK PGCE courses there is separation of primary and secondary. There are so many missed opportunities here. It feels like everyone is digging deeper into their own trench and rarely standing up to look over to the next trench, even though the solution resides there.

Our greatest strength is the exact opposite of specialisation, it is the ability to integrate broadly[7]. For a coaching way of leading we are looking for less isolation and more collaboration and union. We can then begin to enable learning across all areas of your setting, explicitly[8]:

- **People** – acting as a coach and creating a great learning environment
- **Teams** – acting as a facilitator and focusing on drawing out and using the best thinking in teams
- **Institutions** – acting as an integrator and focusing on building the structures and processes needed to best share and use learning across the institution

Trust and Respect

Trust is a key element running through both coaching and leading. The best school leaders build a culture of trust within their organisation through both their competence and their character; crucially, they also demonstrate trust in their staff.

'When you are leading, the success comes not from yourself. It comes from the other people in the organisation,' says Deborah Eyre, Founder of High Performance Learning. In terms of promoting a culture of high performance learning, 'it's a teacher's agenda, it's not something you can mandate from the top.

You have to introduce the ideas and ask the teachers to figure out how to make it work in their context. There's a lot of autonomy in it.'

Brian Cooklin, MD at Nord Anglia education agrees that facilitating autonomy is key. 'Encourage talent, allow staff to develop their own skills. You need to give them that capacity to try different things. When you give staff the autonomy to do something and have that space to build the confidence - of staff and children - you get great results.'

Trust is a key personal characteristic in building relationships and as such is part of ethical leadership. In the UK this is supported by a *Framework for Ethical Leadership in Education*[9] providing the profession with the principles to support leaders in their decision making. Leaders need to be trustworthy and reliable, holding trust on behalf of children, and should be beyond reproach. Leaders can engender trust through being reliable, consistent, humble, courageous and kind as well as having a genuine interest in people. Activate your Fundamental coaching skills to develop rapport through deep listening and try to get to know your people for who they are[10].

Damian Hughes, author and Professor of Organisational Psychology and Change at Manchester Metropolitan University, narrows it down to three demonstrable behaviours:

- knowledge (and therefore credibility)
- energy
- integrity

Hughes asks, 'Do you role model the behaviours you're asking everyone else to do? Ambiguity is the enemy. If you're unclear about the behaviours you expect or they're too numerous people won't understand.'

Dialogue is particularly relevant when seeking to build a climate of trust, a space in which new possibilities are most likely to emerge through effective communication[11]. US studies[12] found that improvement in communication will only occur when both trust and respect are present. Fidler[13] offers an illustration of the relevance of this (see diagram below) citing improvement only when both trust and respect are present, key elements of the coaching relationship itself. This also has huge parallels with instructional coaching and teacher development. Notice the type of energy on show, whether catabolic or anabolic and energy blocks, such as limiting beliefs, and interpretations when connecting with people and navigating relationships.

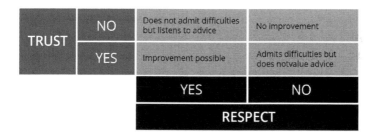

TRUST	NO	Does not admit difficulties but listens to advice	No improvement
	YES	Improvement possible	Admits difficulties but does notvalue advice
		YES	NO
		RESPECT	

Developing Relationships Through Dialogue

In education most of us tend to gravitate towards a 'telling' mode. As a leader, I know I am in telling mode when I find myself convinced that my way is the right way, and that anyone who disagrees is resistant to change. As a coach, I know I am in telling mode when I find myself convinced I know the answer. When we find ourselves in these states we are engaged in 'monologue'.

If we want to lead more successfully, more often, we need to get better at engaging in 'dialogue'[14]. Dialogue is discussed in the Transformative domain (in Part 1), in particular Amanda Riding's observation[15] about balancing advocacy and enquiry. Advocacy can be a telling mode, enquiry involves holding ambiguity, difference and uncertainty and rummaging around in them for fresh connections, for new information or insights[16]. At the mastery stage of dialogue, you act as a co-reflective partner, enhancing people's reflective capacity and sense of identity and so allowing them to more fully take meaning from events[17].

A leader's role is not always to get the results *per se*, it is to ensure that the people they are working with can achieve them. Rather than focussing solely on leadership skills and competencies, we need to utilise our Transformative dialogue skills which enable us to influence and engage more effectively.

A new human-centred approach to learning would put the person at the heart of the learning goals, not the job they do. This would help us to stop defining people simply as their job, their position in a hierarchy, or their salary cost. We are all so much more than that[18]. 'People are craving depth and human to human connection now more than ever, meaning the expectation is rising for authenticity, vulnerability, and relationship-based interactions'[19].

There is a paradox in leaders letting people get on and do their job whilst also connecting with them on a deeper level than they may have previously. Professor Erik de Haan shares the following key insights into why leaders must open up new conversations to bring the best out of the people and teams they are working with[20].

By drawing on your increased awareness and overall coaching evolution you can:
- take a step back and observe yourself in interactions
- keep close to your staff to check if you are having the right kind of conversation and how you could help them more
- take a step back to work through issues that rise, hold the agenda and a secure space for your staff

The challenge is to relinquish the idea that you need to be clear about how to solve a problem, or even know what technique to use to help a colleague to do so, so providing an opening for a collaborative conversation where new understanding can emerge. This is working in the space between, as explored in Transformative coaching[21].

As a leader, at times you are required to enact 'soft power' when developing relationships. This is the power of friendly persuasion rather than command, to expand sphere of influence22. At other times you will need to be more straightforward to get the best out of people. Steve Radcliffe calls this robust dialogue[23]: direct conversation that gets to the truth of the matter without shying away from saying what needs to be said or taking things personally. Look to build the relationships that can allow robust dialogue to happen.

Creating the conditions for dialogue

The essential task of a leader or leadership team is to lead the co-creation of a space in which people are able to support each other's learning[24].

I believe dialogue needs practice. Think of it as developing a new skill, rather than simply turning up and hope for the best. For example, I hear from leaders about the responsibility they feel for initiating dialogue in team meetings, keeping items moving forward and ensuring everyone is involved and informed.

Your role as a leader is to provide a container – a safe and supportive environment that encourages openness and trust among participants[25]. A container is a setting in which deep and transformative listening becomes possible; a holding space where the potential for shared understanding can manifest[26]. As a leader this could encapsulate overall working with your teams or departments, or a meeting which draws on your coaching evolution.

Let us unpick how you go about fashioning the conditions for effective leadership conversations and dialogue.

Preparation

This is about preparing the setting and routines for dialogue. Draw on the overview of contracting outlined in the Fundamental domain, including being clear on the basics including: location, seating positions, purpose, roles and behaviour expectations.

Think about:

- The actual space where the dialogue is happening. Does this need to be on site or off site for example?
- Do you want to sit in a circle to promote openness?
- Would you like to have refreshments available throughout the meeting?

Set the conditions to deliver fruitful dialogue by preparing your 'way of being' including the centre, widen and listen' grounding as outlined in Transformative coaching.

Building the container

In setting up the space and environment to engage in fruitful dialogue you will bring together themes from each coaching domain:

Fundamental

A good start is to check in, perhaps by opening with a question to ignite conversation, as in the BASIC coaching model[27]. You will need to draw upon Fundamental coaching skills here, including active listening and questioning, whilst facilitating dialogue. Notice the energy blocks such as limiting beliefs and challenge accordingly.

Systemic

Refer to the Systemic coaching domain to understand and explore wider themes through the six lenses of team coaching[28]: individual, inter-personal, team tasks, team relationships, stakeholder interfaces and wider systemic context.

Transformative

Draw on the Transformative domain's five dimensions of dialogue[29] to evoke the ideal, support dreaming out loud, deepen the listening, make it safe for opposers and dare to suspend.

Managing the container

Throughout dialogic interactions there is collective responsibility to guide and manage the conversations, to notice patterns at play and provide guidance when required. This might be the role of the leader, a range of people, or even someone facilitating the session. You also need to hold the space for fruitful dialogue to happen, aligning with the non-formal approach to teaching where you are facilitating learning.

The whole process is illustrated in the diagram below[30].

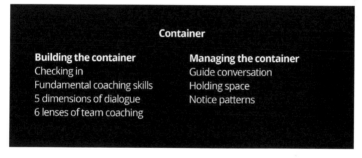

Review

Reflecting on the themes emerging from the dialogue and how they will impact future thinking. A reflective framework such as Kolb's model,[31] shown in the diagram overleaf, can be a good way to structure dialogue here.

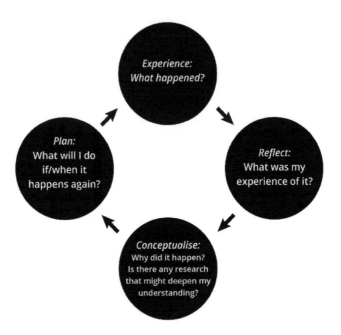

Experience:
What happened?

Reflect:
What was my experience of it?

Conceptualise:
Why did it happen?
Is there any research
that might deepen my
understanding?

Plan:
What will I do
if/when it
happens again?

Example:

When visiting a school in Russia we utilised the above process as part of a senior boarding school team training on how to improve communication and ways of working.

The preparation stage was quite straight forward – we had a lot of space to use because students had not yet returned from summer holidays. We decided on a circle seating plan, with breaks planned throughout the morning. Language was a potential barrier so we translated expectations into Russian to ensure everyone was clear on how we would operate. This included basic expectations such as speaking and listening as well as outlining the five dimensions of dialogue to provide a steer to the discussions. We wanted to make it clear that alternative opinions were welcomed articulated in the right manner.

In the container stage we incorporated the six lenses of team coaching to provide an agenda. This helped everyone to understand each other's role and that of the team, with wider stakeholder interfaces. We also experimented with some group coaching action learning sets: people brought their challenges to the table and others coached them on these. With this shared understanding we were able to begin to design a team identity, unpicking shared values, symbols, rituals, language and guiding principles.

I facilitated the conversations alongside a Russian member of staff to provide language support and cultural knowhow.
We finally used the reflective model to review the session. The feedback was positive, with some people wanting to take the template to try with their own teams. They even wanted to use the reflective model with students inside the boarding houses to support homework and academic progression.

Building Teams

The future of leadership is organic, a development away from a single leader of any persuasion to a focus on networks of groups and teams. Hierarchies will increasingly be phased out, with people not having an over-dependency on the leader[32].

Collective leadership will shift the focus from the leader as an individual to the connections between team members engaging in the wider context33. This aligns with both Systemic and Transformative coaching, with the focus progressing to the functioning of social networks rather than prescribed systems and models.

To build effective teams you need to draw on the coaching skills and approaches found in the Fundamental domain. These include[34]:

- listening
- questioning
- giving feedback
- summarising and paraphrasing

- being open about feelings
- collaboration
- communication
- managing conflict
- managing meetings
- enabling learning

As we know, building a team requires contracting, setting the team rules if you like. Sometimes, as a leader your presence alone is enough to influence thinking and opinion so, drawing on the 'flip learning' model, get your team to first discuss issues without you being in the room. Then take input from your team and make a decision. This is not collaborative decision making, it is options based, generated by a team, and the final decision sits with you, the leader. This approach promotes ownership, the group become self-governing. You know you have cracked it when things run themselves and this then becomes the team culture.

'The best teams also have cognitive diversity,' says René Carayol MBE, a leading executive coach who works with government leaders, FTSE 100 and Fortune 500 CEOs. To facilitate and encourage teamwork between staff members, 'leaders need to find more leaders – people who can influence and persuade, regardless of their role or title.' He reminds us that this applies to your senior leadership team too: 'Do not travel so far you can't hear a dissenting voice – listen to them.'

As a group or team coach you need to create the conditions for coaching to work; so too should you do this in the way that you lead. Important elements for building an effective team are[35]:

- alignment of purpose in relation to value, beliefs and identity
- psychological safety where people can be honest and have robust conversations
- team learning in which best practice is shared

Peter Hawkins goes into a little more detail[36] and talks about how leaders can develop a team through five disciplines:

- Commission: why are we all here? What is the purpose of the team and stakeholders' expectations?
- Clarifying: what are we going to be doing that can only be completed by members of the team working collectively?
- Co-creating: how will you work together as a unit to generate new thinking and ways of operating?
- Connecting: how do you connect with stakeholders outside of the team? How do you represent the team when you are dealing with different people and systems in your setting?
  Core learning: in light of the commission, clarifying, co-creating and connecting, how is the team doing? When does the team craft opportunities to reflect and develop?

These five disciplines form a fantastic agenda for a team meeting, particularly for a new team or one that is resetting at the start of an academic year, for example. You can also use the five as part of the container process outlined earlier in this chapter. As a leader, asking someone to facilitate the meeting can be more beneficial than leading it yourself, to better allow you to feed into the discussion. I now employ this tactic in my university work and it is an approach that I wished I had implemented when leading schools.

Once you have begun to develop your team you can also draw on Fundamental coaching domain models to run effective team meetings (something I incorporated in developing meetings when working in an international school in Cairo). The easy-to-remember structure brings consistency and allows meetings to run in your absence (which hadn't happened previously in my experience).

Example:

The CLEAR model

Contracting: what do we want to get done in the meeting today and how do we need to work collectively to achieve this?

Listening: before we explore issues and challenges, let's listen to everyone's perspectives and points of view.

Exploring: let's now explore the elements needed to forward the action from the meeting today.

Action: what will we now do and by when?

Review: Close the session by asking what went well and even better if.

Whether building teams or running team meetings, collaboration and psychological safety are key factors[37]. They allow people to honestly feed into discussions and be secure enough to question opinions and direction.

Collaboration

There is a meeting that sticks in my mind from my time leading an international school in the US. There was frustration from staff that, in an effort to demonstrate collegiality and trust, the leadership team had established teacher committees for committees' sake and nothing of substance was actually being achieved. In essence, staff wanted the leadership team to be more decisive, make decisions and set direction for the future. Looking back, they were right.

It seems, now more than ever, that employee ownership and servant leadership is being posited as the optimal way to run an organisation. Karen Legge describes it as 'developmental humanism'[38]; treating the employee as a valued asset, proactive rather than passive, engaged not distant, worthy of trust and commitment. However, Jacky Lumby[39] argues that if collegiality and ownership were the only way, it would condemn many educational organisations to paralysis.

Through the leadership coaching and development work I undertake, I often support clients through the process of collaboration, exploring when to open up discussion and when to make decisions and move things forward. Hitting the collaborative 'sweet spot', so to speak, could then be seen to be a key determinant of leadership effectiveness.

Categories of collaboration

I would like to offer Carol Cardno's categories of collaboration model[40] as a strategic tool when leading a school.

Cardno outlines five progressive stages:

1. Information: letting people know
2. Consultation: seeking response
3. Discussion: facilitating debate
4. Involvement: inviting people
5. Participation: taking a full part

This model can provide a steer when planning collaboration. When, for example, is it time for disseminating information – letting people know of developments as opposed to opening discussion and facilitating a debate? When is it best to invite people to contribute to planning, instead of taking a full part in strategic formulation?

In my own coaching experience, it is common for leaders to fall into one of two camps. In the first, the leader tends to shy away from actively seeking collaboration. This could be for fear of looking vulnerable, opening up the possibility that they are not in control or, indeed, are not experts in every situation. These leaders generally work in the initial stages of Cardno's model (information and consultation), letting people know and seeking response without inviting further involvement.

In the second camp are leaders at the other end of the spectrum, asking for too much involvement in issues that may not necessitate full participation. This may be due to lack of confidence, an inability to make effective decisions, or even not wanting to become unpopular. These leaders tend to operate in the latter stages of Cardno's model (involvement and participation) without accessing and utilising earlier stages fully.

Using this model to plot activities and situations most aligned to the progressive stages can give guidance and kindle reflection when planning collaboration across a team or organisation. Getting people involved, taking ownership and feeling connected to the vision of an organisation can drive productivity and lay the foundations for success. Being strategic about when and how to collaborate can go a long way towards supporting this process.

Psychological Safety

Psychological safety is a shared belief amongst individuals as to whether it is safe to engage in interpersonal risk-taking in the workplace[41]. The fundamentals of psychological safety encapsulate freedom to express ideas and opinions within inclusive environments that garner constructive criticism and dissent. People are confident enough to say 'I don't know'. Psychological safety is about trust, to show vulnerability in discussing mistakes and be able to offer robust feedback. Think also of 'holding' in terms of someone's agenda and space as discussed in Part 1. This is leadership that is ego-minimised and adaptive.

A positive team climate is the most important driver of psychological safety and most likely to occur when leaders demonstrate supportive, consultative behaviours. They do this by being catalysts, empowering and enabling other leaders on the team to help cultivate psychological safety by role modelling and reinforcing the behaviours they expect from the rest of the team[42].

For professional rugby referee, Sara Cox, psychological safety is a key element in relation to working in tandem with her team: 'I need to provide an environment for my match team to feel comfortable in challenging me, be a part of that game and really buy in to the flow of what's happening.'

Developing psychological safety

There are many ways to develop team climate and bonding. When working with teams I find that being creative – undertaking engaging experiences that people remember – can support the development of psychological safety. As well as incorporating music into sessions, I also use LEGO. Institute for Management Development (IMD) professors created the LEGO 'serious play' concept in 1996 as a way to enable managers to solve problems, explore ideas and achieve objectives[43].

Essentially, participants build LEGO models representing their ideas or reflections. The models serve as a basis for further group discussion and knowledge sharing, as opposed to responding with words as in traditional coaching conversations[44].

Example:

I led a coaching fundamentals session in Kuwait with a group of senior leaders from across a range of school sites. The first task was to work in pairs to build a LEGO model that represented what coaching meant to them. This was followed by using Fundamental coaching skills, such as questioning, to draw feedback from participants.

As well as engaging the group, it had the effect of strengthening bonds between people in an immersive way, so helped the breaking down of barriers, allowing people to express themselves in a non-threatening way.

Building LEGO models to describe situations, people's strengths, or a shared vision, can help to build trust. Start with a focus on individual modelling, how each person interprets the 'thing' in the spotlight. Then progress to a shared modelling activity to illustrate what it looks like from a plurality of viewpoints.

Finally you can illustrate system modelling, demonstrating viewpoints from across a whole school or sector. I invite you to be inventive!

High Value Teams

Professor Deborah Eyre, academic researcher and founder of High Performance Learning, which supports schools of all types to become high performing, defines high performance as, 'what people do at the optimal level - what does the very best look like? High performance is what you see when you've got optimal learning occurring.'

Liz Free, CEO and Director of International School Rheintal, Switzerland and Founding Director of the International Leadership Academy, identifies high performance as, 'in its simplest form, sustained progress over time' whereas Kim Green, Head of School at International School, Ho Chi Minh City, Vietnam takes a more teacher-centric view: 'High performance means individuals are flourishing, displaying compassion and can engage in innovation.'

'I want my staff to continue a love of learning,' says Irfan Latif, Principal of DLD College, London, a 14-19 boarding and day school that was awarded UK Boarding School of the Year 2020. 'It's all about coaching. We feel that by giving our students the ability to be coached by our staff and our staff to have those coaching skills, does lead to high performing teams within our school environment, whether in academic departments, in pastoral teams, in the house system or overall as a school.'

There is also a view that high performing teams is an outdated concept that grew out of 20th-century mechanistic linear thinking, a focus on efficiency rather than creating benefit for all stakeholders. In the same way that we can move from Fundamental towards Transformative approaches in coaching (and away from formal approaches in teaching), we can also progress from a high-performance team to teams of high value. Teams of high value are rooted in systemic ways of seeing the world; these teams co-create value with all stakeholders built on collaboration and co-adaptability, rather than competition45.

In his work on reinventing organisations, Frederic Laloux posits the emergence of a new organisational model he named 'Teal'[46], identifying three breakthroughs in new organisations:

- Self-management: this is peer-to-peer and team led without the need for hierarchy
- Wholeness: moving past a narrow professional self to embrace all parts of people in the organisation
- Evolutionary purpose: the organisation has a life and direction of its own in a fluid development

Teal requires a shift away from old paradigms to an evolution in consciousness in the way we manage organisations, more in line with a living system or living organism where inner 'rightness' is the guiding compass. This is about shifting away from a hyper-masculine way of operating to a balance of healthy structures, with the spaciousness to flow and feel creative. This has a ripple effect on how we work in schools, as a powerful tool for transformation, healing, and change[47]. Examples of this are outlined in a coaching way of teaching (Part 2).

Developing team-led leadership

During my podcast conversation with him, the Leinster and former England Rugby Head Coach, Stuart Lancaster, describes leadership as being about balancing the need to keep control whilst also letting go. In order to create ownership and have an effective team he believes you need to go through the following process[48]:

1. Culture
The first stage is to get the right people in the right positions to promote the values and behaviours you are looking for.

2. Identity
Connect to the history of the school or setting in which you are working. For older institutions there may well be a visible history to connect to, whilst in start-ups this is more about step 3.

3. Higher purpose
Look beyond targets and results to unpick your overall purpose. This can link to mission, culture and identity.

4. Behaviour and standards
Your higher purpose informs the requisite behaviours and standards of working.

5. Ownership
When everyone is aware of the culture (expected values and behaviours required) then ownership begins to develop.

6. Leadership
Once ownership is in place you then have team-led leadership; this is the last piece in the jigsaw when every other stage has been activated.

Summary

Relationships are the second stage towards implementing a coaching way of leading. This builds on developing your self-awareness. You can begin to develop this area through:

- Enhance communication by utilising your Fundamental domain coaching skills to developing positive social relationships in your setting.
- Build a culture of trust and respect by demonstrating behaviours that provide you with credibility and integrity.
- Create the right conditions to foster effective dialogue through building a dialogic container drawing on your coaching skills.
- Building high value teams by promoting psychological safety and collaboration.

References

1. Radcliffe, S. (2012) Leadership Plain and Simple, FT Publishing, UK
2. Pendleton, D. & Furnham, A. (2012) Leadership, All You Need to Know, Palgrave
3. Lawrence, P. (2021), Reinventing leadership, (https://systems5ways.com/wp-content/uploads/2021/02/Systems-for-leaders.pdf)
4. Shaked, H. & Schechter, C. (2020) Systemic Thinking Leadership: New Explorations for School Improvement in Management in Education, Vol.34, No.3, July 2020
5. West-Burnham, J. (1997) Managing Quality in Schools, Pearson Education, UK
6. Goldman, D. (2020) Leadership That Gets Results, Harvard Business Review, March & April 2020
7. Epstein, D. (2019) Range: How Generalists Triumph in a Specialized World, Macmillan, US
8. McFarland, W. & Goldsworthy, S. (2014) Choosing Change, McGraw Hill, US
9. ASCL (2019) Framework for ethical leadership in education, (www.ascl.org.uk/Help-and-Advice/Leadership-and-governance/Strategic-planning/Framework-for-ethical-leadership-in-education)
10. Uttley, J. (2019) Ethical Leadership: I Like It. What Is It? (https://trustleadership.wordpress.com/2019/03/31/ethical-leadership-i-like-it-what-is-it/)
11. Lawrence, P. (2021) Group Coaching, A Powerful Intervention, White Paper Feb 2021, Centre for Coaching in Organisations, Australia
12. Salaman, L. (1991) in Middlewood, D. (1997) in Bush, T. & Middlewood, D. (1997) Managing People in Education, Paul Chapman Publishing, UK
13. Fidler, B. (1995), in Middlewood, D (1997) in Bush, T. & Middlewood, D. (1997) Managing People in Education, Paul Chapman Publishing, UK
14. Lawrence, P. (2021) Group Coaching, A Powerful Intervention, White Paper Feb 2021, Centre for Coaching in Organisations, Australia
15 & 16. Ridings, A. (2011) Pause for Breath, Live it Publishing, UK
17. Stelter, R. (2017) The Art of Dialogue in Coaching, Routledge, UK
18. Broadbelt, G. (2021) Finding The Human Connection Between Learning and Performance (www.impactinternational.com/blog/2021/03/finding-human-connection-between-learning-and-performance?utm_campaign=249&utm_source=InGoodCompany&utm_medium=email&utm_content=Finding%20the%20human%20connection%20between%20learning%20and%20performance&jujrtyghfud50966a7503912a579a6392a13226a13494)
19. Da Costa, C. (2020) Conscious Leadership: Why It's More Important Than Ever (www.forbes.com/sites/celinnedacosta/2020/09/29/conscious-leadership-why-its-more-important-than-ever/?sh=6184a3ad1ecc)
20. De Haan, E. (www.hult.edu/en/executive-education/insights/leadership-vuca-world/)

21. Knights, A. (2021) Why Leaders Who Coach Are More Important Now Than Ever (www.hult.edu/en/executive-education/insights/why-coaching-leaders-are-important/?utm_source=linkedin&utm_medium=social&utm_campaign=organicsociallinkedin&utm_content=openprograms)

22. Winder, R. (2020) Soft Power: The New Great Game, Little Brown Publishing, US

23. Radcliffe, S. (2012) Leadership Plain and Simple, FT Publishing, UK

24. Lawrence, P. (2021) Group Coaching, A Powerful Intervention, White Paper Feb 2021, Centre for Coaching in Organisations, Australia

25. Thomson, B. (2013) Non-directive Coaching, Critical Publishing Limited, UK

26. Ridings , A. (2011) Pause for Breath, Live it Publishing, UK

27. Buck, A. (2020) The BASIC Coaching Model, Cadogan Press, UK

28. Leary-Joyce, J. & Lines, H. (2018) Systemic Team Coaching, AoEC Press, UK

29. Issacs, W. (1999) in Lawrence, P., Hill, S., Priestland, A., Forrestal, C., Rommerts, F., Hyslop, I. & Manning, M. (2019) The Tao of Dialogue, Routledge Focus, UK

30. Adapted from Beanacre model in Lawrence, P., Hill, S., Priestland, A., Forrestal, C., Rommerts, F., Hyslop, I. & Manning, M. (2019) The Tao of Dialogue, Routledge Focus, UK

31. Kolb, D. (1984) Kolb's Learning Styles and Experiential Learning Cycle, (www.simplypsychology.org/learning-kolb.html)

32. Avery, G. (2004) in Pendleton, D. & Furnham, A. (2012), Leadership, All You Need to Know, Palgrave

33. Leary-Joyce, J. & Lines, H. (2018) Systemic Team Coaching, AoEC Press, UK

34. West-Burnham, J. (1997) Managing Quality in Schools, Pearson Education, UK

35. Widdowson, L. & Barbour, P. (2021) Systemic Team Coaching in Passmore, J (2021) The Coaches' Handbook, Routledge UK

36. Hawkins, P. (2020) Systemic Coaching, Routledge, UK

37. Wheeler, S., Gold, R. & Passmore. J. (2020) All To Play For: LEGO® SERIOUS PLAY® and Its Impact on Team Cohesion, Collaboration and Psychological Safety in Organisational Settings Using a Coaching Approach, Emerald Publishing, UK

38. Legge, K. (2005) in Human Resource Management, in Whitehead, S. (2012) Keele tutor notes, Keele University, UK

39. Lumby, J. (1998) Understanding Strategic Change, in Middlewood, D. & Lumby, J. (2004) Strategic Management in Schools and Colleges, Paul Chapman Publishing, Sage Publications, London

40. Cardno, C. (2012) Managing Effective Relationships in Education, Sage, UK

41. Edmondson et al. (2007) Edmondson & Lei, 2014; Newman et al., 2017, in Wheeler, S,. Gold, R. & Passmore. J (2020) All To Play For: LEGO® SERIOUS PLAY® and its Impact on Team Cohesion, Collaboration and Psychological Safety in Organisational Settings Using a Coaching Approach, Journal of Work Applied Management, July 2020

42. De Smet, A. (2021) Psychological Safety and the Critical Role of Leadership Development, (www.mckinsey.com/business-functions/organization/our-

insights/psychological-safety-and-the-critical-role-of-leadership-development?cid=soc-web#)

43. Blair, S. & Rillo, M. (2016) Serious Work, ProMeet, US

44. Wheeler, S., Gold, R. & Passmore. J. (2020) All To Play For: LEGO® SERIOUS PLAY® and Its Impact on Team Cohesion, Collaboration and Psychological Safety in Organisational Settings Using a Coaching Approach, Emerald publishing, UK

45. Hawkins, P. (2020) We Need to Move Beyond High Performing Teams, LinkedIn 5 July 2020, (www.linkedin.com/pulse/we-need-move-beyond-high-performing-teams-professor-peter-hawkins)

46. Laloux, F. (2014) Reinventing Organizations, Nelson Parker, US

47. Da Costa, C. (2020) Conscious Leadership: Why It's More Important Than Ever, (www.forbes.com/sites/celinnedacosta/2020/09/29/conscious-leadership-why-its-more-important-than-ever/?sh=6184a3ad1ecc)

48. Lancaster, S. (www.stuartlancaster.com/leadership)

Part Three: Chapter 3

Agility

Future leaders need to be like the explorers of old and embrace the unknown. They need to be open to new ideas, and change course as the world around them evolves[1]. Agility is about drawing together ways to be able to deal with complexity. You will develop the ability to communicate ideas and interact through relationships with others[2] (as discussed in previous chapters).

According to the results of a 2020 Agile Organisation survey[3], 90% of people said that agility is more important to their success than it was five years ago, whilst 95% of mangers said agility is more important to their organisational success.

Agility in this context involves:

- developing agility and thriving under pressure
- strategic agility
- dancing through change
- leading change

Developing Agility

In today's complex, interconnected and rapidly changing world, the demands placed on our leaders and organisations have grown exponentially[4]. We hear increasingly about the 'Fourth Industrial Revolution', a super-fast transformation of society, technology and consumer expectations that all organisations must address if they are to remain successful. *Everyone* must adapt and respond to these complex challenges[5]. Arguably, leadership has not kept pace with the changing nature of organisations and the leaders they need[6].

According to Dr Haywood's Agile Leadership Model[7] agility can be learned through:

- Seeking opportunities to learn: examples are attending online learning programmes, critical design presentations or 'in house' workshops.
- Creating space to reflect and learn: A key component in learning is the ability to reflect on practice. Does your leadership prioritise crafting the time to stop, pause and reflect?
- Using feedback to fuel learning: Gathering information from multiple locations to provide a clear basis on which to launch subsequent conversations, to help fuel learning and inform planning.

Thriving Under Pressure

A recent UK conference of the International Coaching Federation (ICF) was themed *Remaining Coaching*. Dr Laura Watkins delivered a keynote titled *Neuroscience To Go Beyond*. Discussions centred on incorporating neuroscience into coaching to help leaders to thrive under pressure, develop and adapt to situations.

Research suggests that a first step in cultivating these behaviours lies with fostering a strong brain, through developing personal agility and enhancing self-awareness to notice what we are thinking and feeling.

Personal agility toolkit

Promoting personal agility necessitates setting leaders up with 'brain-friendly' environments. Using your coaching skills, you can help cultivate a strong brain by possessing an awareness of and engaging with five key areas:

- Head: thoughts and focus, e.g., growth mindset and visualisations
- Heart: emotions, e.g., harnessing emotions, emotional labelling and gratitude
- Breath: deliberate breathing or attention, e.g., mindfulness, meditation, breath control and counting
- Body: internal attention or movement, e.g., yoga, shape making and exercise
- Hand: writing or making, e.g., inspirational activities

How does this work in practice?

Begin with assessing how you (the leader) are currently engaged with the five toolkit areas, as above. Is there a prevalence for a particular point or is there an under- or overuse of certain areas? What area might it be more fruitful for you to explore and why?

In further sessions unpick the areas that you (the leader) would like to focus on to develop agility and promote healthy performance going forward, and set action plans in motion to ensure these happen. The implementation of the actions can spread across days, weeks or months dependent on the situation.

Example: monthly plan

- January – Hand: expressive writing through journaling
- February – Breath: taking pulse, calming down and mindfulness techniques
- March – Hand: ringfencing time to play the piano
- April – Head: mindset, don't forget priorities

Rapid cycle learning

A quick and easy way to track progress can be to focus on learnings and intentions as part of a daily review:

- Learnings: What I learnt yesterday (focusing on what you learnt about yourself)
- Intentions: Your intentions for today (and how you will ensure these are implemented)

Incorporating the personal agility toolkit and rapid cycle learning are helpful, practical ways to create an environment that supports a strong brain and enhance the performance of school leaders.

Strategic Agility

Strategy can be defined as the direction and scope of an organisation over the long term, which achieves advantage in a changing environment through its configuration of resources and competences with the aim of fulfilling stakeholder expectations[8].

The best leaders I work with are those who are able to have a broad strategic vision that is both flexible and nuanced. Strategies, in other words, have to form as well as be formulated[9], being system wide. As in the evolution of coaching skills and implementations, it is necessary to move past linear, models-based one-to-one approaches to create a coaching culture and broader unions.

When I was leading schools I remember the amount of time spent in meetings, developing our improvement strategies. I always found these to be great fun and very creative. After a series of meetings, research, feedback and discussions we decided on an **intended strategy**. As this was rolled out inevitably some of the planning was found to be unfit for purpose for whatever reason, becoming **unrealised strategy.**

The elements that were kept in place were **deliberate strategy.** As plans progressed, **emergent strategies** were highlighted as we progressed, based on feedback and changes in situation and circumstance. This is illustrated in the diagram opposite[10].

Strategy development is about probing and responding to circumstances. It is the amalgamation of **emergent strategies** and **deliberate strategies** that finally become a **realised strategy.** Emergent strategies are not necessarily 'bad' and deliberate 'good', but it is an awareness of these that is key and so the agility to be responsive.

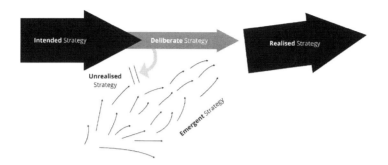

The concept of emergent patterns de-emphasises the directive role of managers, their rationality and their power and therefore poses questions about whether or not management really have control over strategic direction[11]. We live and work in a world so interconnected that linear notions of problem-solving, goals, targets and five-year plans can fail to serve us well[12]. At the heart of the meetings I describe above was coaching methodology, developing the environment and coaching skills necessary to develop emergent themes.

Dancing Through Change

A lot has been written about the volatile, uncertain, chaotic and ambiguous (VUCA) world we live in; it is certainly emblematic of the global pandemic. In this turbulent context, the responsibilities placed on school leaders at all levels have increased, and the need to support leadership is paramount.

Recent research has consistently shown that school leaders are powerful players who can influence school effectiveness and bring about change[13]. To navigate change requires a transformative and paradoxical outlook[14]. Change is constant and, although uncomfortable at times, rarely happens without also bringing opportunity.
Understanding the paradox of change, and learning to be agile, are key components for leading development, helping individuals, teams, groups and organisations collectively move forward in a fast-paced

environment. In the same way that there is a tension between directive and non-directive coaching approaches, there is also a potential paradox between being an enabler and a disruptor in order to influence and lead change.

Enabler

In a sense being an enabler is very much aligned to the idea of transformational leadership. It involves being collegial, creating vision and clarity of direction, empowering and working together. A key element is learning to be agile, dancing rather than stomping through change.

Disruptor

Being a disruptor can be seen to be at odds with the idea of an enabler. We are talking about being bold and decisive, questioning the status quo and creating new ways of thinking and operating. This centres on critical reflection of best practice.

If I reflect on my work developing a PGCE international programme, this idea of enabling and disrupting very much encapsulates our approach for course design and implementation. The approach has been collegial in utilising the talents of a range of educators and professional services teams as well as tapping into peoples' passion and strengths to deliver an outstanding product. In terms of creating new ways of thinking, our mission was to elevate the quality of international teacher training by offering a programme that is more robust, student centred and interactive than our competitors.
It is my view that embracing the contrasting enabler/disruptor roles whilst keeping agile can be key factors in leading change.

Leading Change

In the same way that coaching and education has a bias towards linear, models-based approaches, so in leadership we tend to look for a fast track from problem to solution[15]. The most successful leaders I work with are able to operate differently, in interconnected multi-dimensional ways.

As I've touched upon already, education leaders do not work in fixed policy contexts. Rather, they operate in dynamic educational environments that require them to lead change at school level *and* to connect their schools with opportunities in the wider environment within which they are located and operate[16]. In this multi-dimensional leadership landscape leaders need to be equipped to meet complex demands.

The global Coronavirus pandemic brought these demands into sharp focus. The most striking finding of a School Leadership Supply Crisis report is that almost three-quarters of UK school leaders say the Government's constantly changing guidance was their biggest challenge of the pandemic[17]. Trying to make sense of educational contexts with a single, one-size-fits-all perspective is always likely to be problematic.

Tony Bush talks about leaders needing to develop 'conceptual pluralism', that is selecting the most appropriate approach to a particular issue and avoid a uni-dimensional stance[18].

This is very much aligned to contingency theory which holds that the best way depends on the particular situation and circumstances[19]. The same can be seen in coaching: a toolkit of approaches that can be utilised from Fundamental to Transformative domains.

Daniel Goldman highlights six leadership styles[20]:

- Coercive
- Authoritative
- Affiliative
- Democratic,
- Pace-setting
- Coaching

In short, **coercive** leaders demand compliance; **authoritative** leaders mobilise people towards a vision; **affiliative** leaders create harmony and emotional bonds. **Democratic** leaders develop consensus and participation; **pace-setting** leaders demand excellence and self-direction, and **coaching** leaders develop people for the future.

Choose the appropriate leadership style contingent on the situation or trajectory of the institution you are leading.

A good example of leading change is in the creation of a start-up project, such as a new school. One of my podcast conversations is with the Founding Head of King's College School Chengdu, in China, Mike Seaton, who is clear on the need to be directive and coercive in order to get things in place and have people understand key roles early on.

Choosing Change

In *Choosing Change*, McFarland and Goldsworthy[21] explore a new approach to leading in times of change, outlining what they call the 'Five D framework':

- Disruption
- Desire
- Discipline
- Determination
- Development

This framework could be applied to schools and their leaders looking to increase the effectiveness of both individual and organisational change. Each component of the 'Five D framework' could be used as a model to meet the challenges school leaders are facing.

Disruption

Disruption relates to an event or experience that triggers a conscious choice to change. An obvious example would be the pandemic, an unexpected jolt that has caused huge discomfort and challenged schools, and indeed leaders, to think in different ways. However painful, disruption could be said to be the precursor to growth, learning and development.

Desire

An initial disruption forces leaders and organisations to ask what exactly they want to achieve. Do they believe in the possibility, and how serious are they about making that change happen? Leaders developing self-awareness can enhance this process. Working through coaching energy blocks such as limiting beliefs, interpretations and assumptions can ensure that vision and direction are understood and articulated clearly from both a personal and team-wide perspective. Partnering with a coach can help support this process by working together to establish vision, provide clarity on differing viewpoints as well as tame your inner critic to achieve your goals.

Discipline

Once the desire is clear, it takes discipline, energy and effort to keep developing. This stage is about applying those small, consistent and frequent steps required to build momentum and deliver stainable change. For leaders, it is worth thinking about what that small step looks like each day on the path to achieving your vision. This may necessitate changes in working routines and approach in order to ensure that progress is being made. Once again cultivating self-awareness is key to understanding the best ways forward for you in times of uncertainty. Time to relax and engage in out-of-work activities is essential to recharge.

Determination

Having the resilience to focus and deliver even when faced with setbacks is key to overcoming obstacles on your path to change. Building resilience to enable you to bounce back quickly is an essential element of determination, especially among the potential discomfort brought on by change. For leaders this might encompass exploring ways of switching off from work, keeping healthy in body and energising your mind. Having a growth mindset can help keep you on track to achieve the vision you have formulated in the 'Desire' stage.

Development

School leaders are responsible not only for supporting teachers' and students' development, but also for developing themselves as proactive professionals[22]. Cultivating continuous learning and growth can support your journey towards achieving your vision and goals. This encapsulates creating a climate of feedback, and ongoing learning, both for you the individual and for the organisation. As a leader it is important to identify trusted relationships to support, stretch and challenge you throughout this process, such as a peers or an external resource.

The 'Five D framework' provides a steer for improving your ability to lead both yourself and your organisation through times of change. As with every leadership journey, the first step is to cultivate and develop self-awareness before exercising your leadership muscles through a personal, team and organisational lens.

In times of change the unpredictability of the situation favours a broad leadership repertoire. The broader the repertoire of skills and attributes in a team, the broader range of challenges to which the team is likely to be able to respond successfully. It is worth noting that such a broad repertoire is more likely to be a feature of collective rather than individual leadership[23].

Summary

Developing agility is the final stage towards a coaching way of leading. This builds on developing your self-awareness and relationships. You can begin to develop this area through:

- Learning agility through seeking opportunities to learn, reflect and use feedback to fuel development.
- Incorporate rapid cycle learning to reflect and track progress in relation to developing agility and healthy performance.
- Promote strategic agility through embracing emergent themes as well as deliberate strategies.
- Lead change by enabling and disrupting as well as drawing on models such as the 'Five D framework' to frame strategies.

References

1. Laker, B. (2020) This Is What Leadership Will Be In 2030, (www.forbes.com/sites/benjaminlaker/2020/08/05/this-is-what-leadership-will-be-in-2030/)
2. Widdowson, L. & Barbour, P. (2021) Building Top Performing Teams, KoganPage, UK
3. Wiley, J. (2020) Agile Organisation survey results, Everything Disc, US
4. Wright, A., McLean Walsh, M. & Tennyson, S. (2019) Systemic Coaching Supervision: Responding to the Complex Challenges of our Time, Philosophy of Coaching: An International Journal, Vol.4, No.1
5. Fleming, S. (2020) How Can We Prepare Students for the Fourth Industrial Revolution? (www.weforum.org/agenda/2020/02/schools-of-the-future-report-2020-education-changing-world)
6. Crow, G.M. (2021) in Bailey, L. & Gibson, T. (2019) International School Principals' Routes to Headship and Key Challenges of Their Role, Educational, Management, Administration and Leadership Journal, Vol.48, No.6, Sage, UK
7. Haywood, S. (2017) The Agile Leader, Kogan Page, UK
8. Johnson, G., Scholes, K. & Whittingham, R. (2008) Exploring Corporate Strategy, Prentice Hall, US
9. Mintzberg, H., Ahlstrand, B. & Lampel, J. (2009) Strategy Safari, Prentice Hall, UK
10. Diagram adapted from Mintzberg, H., Ahlstrand, B. & Lampel, J. (2009) Strategy Safari, Prentice Hall, UK

11. Johnson, G., Scholes, K. & Whittingham, R. (2008) Exploring Corporate Strategy, Prentice Hall, US

12. Einzig, H. (2017) The Future of Coaching, Routledge, UK

13. Qadach., M., Schechter, C. & Da'as, R. (2020) Instructional Leadership and Teachers' Intent to Leave, Educational Management, Administration and Leadership Journal, Vol.48, No.4, Sage, UK

14. Haywood, S. (2017)'s The agile leader, Kogan Page, UK

15. Einzig, H. (2017) The future of coaching, Routledge, UK, p. 39

16. Miller, P.W. (2018) The Nature of School Leadership, Intercultural Studies in Education, Palgrave Macmillan, US

17. Davies, R. (2021) Recovery? School Leaders Need It As Much As Their Students, Schools Week (https://schoolsweek.co.uk/recovery-school-leaders-need-it-as-much-as-their-students/)

Bush, T. (2011) Theories of Educational Leadership and Management, Sage, UK

19. Pearson, G. (1999) Strategy in Action, Prentice Hall, Pearson Education Ltd, England

20. Goldman, D. (2020) Leadership That Gets Results, Harvard Business Review, March & April 2020

21. McFarland, W. & Goldsworthy, S. (2014) Choosing Change, McGraw Hill, US

22. Cranston, N. (2013) in Kim, T. (2020) Becoming Skilful Leaders, BELMAS Educational Management Administration and Leadership Journal, Vol.48, No.2, March 2020, Sage, UK

23. Pendleton, D. & Furnham, A. (2012) Leadership, All You Need to Know, Palgrave

Part Three: Chapter 4

A Shift in Leadership

One theme emerging in all my coaching work has been that successful school leaders are becoming more committed to a 'coaching' way of leadership; more importantly they have found their own time (past and present) with a coach has given them the confidence and tools to unlock their own potential for high performance leadership.

A coaching way of leading requires a shift away from old paradigms to an evolution in consciousness in the way we manage organisations. This change necessitates a move away from the current process driven, hierarchical educational approach found in school systems around the world[1]. Most current systems have a narrow focus on targets, growth and efficiency. Our humanity, our human purposes, our relationships, our compassion, our love, our hopes and dreams are all too often left at the door as we enter our workplaces[2].

Organisations, and the leadership of those organisations, can be more in line with a living system or living organism where inner rightness is the guiding compass. Self-organising teams allow strategy to emerge organically in a purpose and values driven culture, where job descriptions are replaced by more fluid roles[3].

Future leaders then, should have: transparency, accountability, diversity and be purpose-driven towards contribution and creativity[4]. Leadership skills should also build on the 'human' side of leadership, including compassion, humility and vulnerability[5]. In my view there is a need for leadership to move from a 'command and control' style to one that has a more engagement, dialogical and coaching style[6]. This is not about being 'fluffy' or 'weak' in your leadership. Coaching is about facilitating change and change can be uncomfortable.

As Professor Damian Hughes quite rightly states: 'Great coaches comfort the troubled and trouble the comfortable.'[7] Coaching and leadership are not for the fainthearted and although the tyrant is in retreat across leadership, the leader who will not be denied, who has expertise coupled with a strength of will is not disappearing anytime soon[8].

In fact, incorporating coaching into our leadership allows us to build confidence and create a climate of leaning into the tough conversations, to bring learning and growth to the places in which we work.

References

1. Laloux, F. (2014) Reinventing Organizations, Nelson Parker, US
2. Broadbelt, G. (2021) Finding The Human Connection Between Learning and Performance (www.impactinternational.com/blog/2021/03/finding-human-connection-between-learning-and-performance?utm_campaign=249&utm_source=InGoodCompany&utm_medium=email&utm_content=Finding%20the%20human%20connection%20between%20learning%20and%20performance&jujrtyghfud50966a7503912a579a6392a13226a13494)
3. Laloux, F. (2014) Reinventing Organizations, Nelson Parker, US
4. Enzig, H. (2017) The Future of Coaching, Routledge, US
5. Culpin, V. (2021) Leadership in the 21st Century – Lessons From a Pandemic, EF Education First and Hult Ashridge Executive Education
6. Hawkins, P. (2012) Creating a Coaching Culture, McGraw Hill, UK
7. McKie, N. (2020) Persyou Inspiring Leadership podcast guest, series 4, episode 8
8. Walsh, B. (2009) The Score Takes Care of Itself, Portfolio Penguin, US

Part Four

Case Studies

My experience across teaching, leading and coaching in education both in the UK and internationally has provided me not only with some fantastic opportunities in my career, but also some valuable insights into how coaching skills and approaches can be implemented. Here, I offer two case studies: real-world examples of coaching ways in the contexts of international teacher recruitment and post-graduate level teacher training development.

Part Four: Chapter 1

A Coaching Way of Teacher Recruitment

In this chapter, I explore the implications for career coaching through a case study in the rapidly expanding international education sector. It takes into account the experiences of coaching at numerous international teacher recruitment events in London, Bangkok and Dubai, working with over 300 school recruiters (education directors and school heads) and in the region of 600 teaching candidates from all over the world.

International Education Context

The 2018 International Schools Consultancy (ISC) Global Report[1] indicated that there were over 9,500 international schools, located in virtually every country in the world.

ISC has predicted that the market will continue to develop at a healthy pace, forecasting that by 2028 the number of international schools will have reached 16,600. The number of students attending international schools will have reached nearly 10 million.

'The biggest challenge for the market is professional capital; maintaining the high skills and qualified teachers. With the number of teachers working in international schools expected to increase from 648,000 in 2023 to 896,000 in 2028, the need to attract more teachers of the calibre demanded by schools is becoming a concern.'[2]

The requirement for recruiting teachers in this sector is forecast to pull a quarter of teachers from the UK, Ireland, US and Australia overseas *each year over the next decade* to meet demand[3]. This is an astonishing number.

An International Education Recruitment Event

The type of international education recruitment event discussed in this case study could be described as exceptionally fast paced, with school recruiters and candidates flying in from all over the world for the two-day duration. The first morning usually consists of a briefing, followed by a sign-up session conducted in an interactive 'market' atmosphere, in which schools advertise vacancies and candidates meet prospective employers.

By the end of the two-hour sign-up session, candidates will hope to have secured interviews with a range of schools, for teaching positions the following academic year. Alongside interviews, schools present to candidates, providing an overview of their specific institution and host country. Events of this kind transitioned to online platforms during the pandemic so the future may be a blended approach.

Coaching is available and delivered throughout the event with candidates accessing this in between sign-up sessions, interviews, networking receptions and presentations. Coaching sessions generally last between five to fifteen minutes in length, mostly single sessions with some candidates revisiting coaching as the recruitment process progresses over the two days. There is generally no prior relationship between candidates and coach.

Coaching Considerations

The key considerations required for coaching in the international education recruitment setting can be summarised into three distinct areas: holistic approach, agile approach and ethical practice.

Holistic approach

In relation to the systemic context of an educational recruitment event, both a micro and macro element can be seen to exist. The recruitment event itself is a micro system whilst the international education sector as a whole is the macro system to which all parties belong.

Within the micro system, political tensions can be found with competing schools coveting the same candidates, alongside the potential bias of the event organisers, who must attract potential candidates to produce fees.

Understanding the systemic discourse can be beneficial for coaches when working with both candidates and recruiters within this type of setting. Alongside the complexity of navigating factors at play in this environment, coaching at an international event necessitates taking into consideration the unique context of the candidates themselves. The sheer diversity of schools and candidates requires a cultural sensitivity and understanding coupled with an ability to work with people from a broad range of countries and backgrounds. Synergising an awareness and understanding of the client's agenda (interpersonal) alongside the knowledge of broader micro and macro systemic considerations (institutional) found in international education recruitment settings are key considerations for a holistic coaching approach.

Agile practice

As discussed in a coaching way of leading (Part 3), Haywood[4] outlines seeking opportunities to learn as a key ingredient in becoming agile. When applied to an international education recruitment event, seeking opportunities to learn requires the coach to immerse themselves in the event with the purpose of understanding the relevant systems. This could require meeting event organisers and attending school presentations, fostering an understanding of the context and agenda behind each stakeholder.

The fast-paced nature of such an event means finding the space to reflect and gather feedback to fuel learning can be difficult. A key consideration for coaches then is how to assess their coaching practice to ascertain its effectiveness and in turn, how to adapt and respond to the needs of their clients (teaching candidates) accordingly. It is worth casting an eye to teaching approaches here for answers in terms of understanding different forms of assessment through both a summative and formative lens.

Coaching assessment

'Summative assessments provide a shared and consistent understanding of achievements through testing large domains of content to be taken in standard conditions'[5]; in short, this is much like an exam or test. Formative assessment refers to all those activities used as feedback to modify the teaching and learning activities in which they are engaged: 'Such assessments become formative when the evidence is actually used to adapt the teaching to meet the needs of students.'[6]

Summative assessment of coaching work can be gleaned at the end of an international education recruitment event. To use another teaching phrase, utilise 'What went well? And even better if…' debrief sessions with event organisers. In addition, daily self-reflection on themes emerging from the coaching can help provide useful information to take into the following day. In the same way that formative feedback can be key to effective teaching, this feedback approach can help refine and develop effective coaching in education recruitment settings. A simple reflection on what was useful with the client at the end of a short coaching session can help steer practice and ensure it is fit for purpose. Being responsive and coaching critically, reflecting 'in action' as opposed to 'on action'[7] can ensure coaching efforts are effective in the 'now' and with subsequent clients throughout the event.

Directive and non-directive coaching

One-off coaching sessions are delivered in short periods of time at these recruitment events, so it is essential to get to issues quickly and set conversations in context concisely. A good foundation for coaching in this setting is the ability to shift from directive (mentoring in nature) to non-directive (coaching in nature) approaches when required (as outlined in the Fundamental coaching domain in Part 1).

Contingency coaching

In addition to being able to incorporate a range of approaches, coaching at an international education recruitment event requires skills from a variety of different coaching niches. By this, I mean the ability to switch focus from, for example, relocation to career progression or leadership to wellness coaching, all within the same short session. In this multi-faceted coaching paradigm being agile enough to work within different niches is beneficial for coaches – and candidates!

As explored in Part 3, Bush[8] outlines the concept of 'contingency leadership' as adopting a specific leadership style most effective to the situation at hand. Perhaps 'contingency coaching' acknowledges the uniquely diverse nature of an international education recruitment event, requiring a carefully selected mode of responsiveness. There are parallels with teaching approaches in the informal way of teaching – generalists with a breadth of perspective and the ability to connect the proverbial dots.

Ethical practice

With a multitude of competing systems in play at international education recruitment events, the ethical discourse can be a difficult one to navigate at times. A coaching goal can be to display a non-biased approach: helping clients to learn rather than teaching them[9]. Professional objectivity can be hard to manage. Is it ethical and in the best interests of the candidate to potentially influence a decision or, more commonly, be directive when asked about a specific institution? Conversely, conflict of interest may arise, such as influencing candidates to take up a position at a school that is well known, has a positive reputation or indeed is an institution with which the coach or event staff have links.

Exploiting any aspect of the coaching relationship for professional, personal or monetary advantage is in breach of the International Coaching Federation code of ethics[10]. Coaches also need to be aware of personal assumptions; just because a school has an excellent reputation, will it continue to do so in the future? Major life, relocation and career decisions are made at these events and whether anyone's remit is to influence decisions either way is a point for further reflection. A coach with a background in international education, whilst being helpful in terms of credibility and an understanding of the context and systems, can also raise a number of ethical considerations.

Coaching Challenges in this Setting

Taking the above into consideration, it could be argued that flexibility of approach is the core challenge for a coach working at international education recruitment events.

Firstly, an awareness of the holistic overview and systemic discourse is required; that is, the micro recruitment event system and the macro dimension of international education and diversity of coachees. Secondly, being able to work within a plurality of coaching niches systematically, incorporating a variety of coaching skills underpinned by assessment, to adapt practice accordingly. Thirdly, working within all of the above under significant time constraints.

The International Coaching Federation Core Competencies outline the foundations of a coaching approach as establishing the coaching agreement with trust and intimacy[11]. The nature of coaching at these events, however, throws up challenges for initial contracting and building relationships. Quickfire sessions, with limited time for deep connection, are common. 'So much of a successful coaching relationship is based on chemistry and trust, and how quickly this can be established.'[12] How then can relationships be forged and trust established in order to provide real benefit to coachees?

Perhaps the nature of coaching at these events is not about true transformation in its purest sense, but something on a transactional level. Certainly the coach needs to connect quickly with the coachee, which is perhaps why a coach with strong international education credentials and experience could be seen to foster trust from the outset. But the biggest challenge for a coach with background knowledge is to be fully aware of the ethical considerations and remain in an impartial place. 'A perpetual challenge for a coach is to remain in a state of not knowing, as being in the role of 'expert' can lead coaches to diagnose and find solutions, which may not be what the client needs.'[13]

A way forward: three coaching stages

There is precedence for one-off coaching work through the Single Session Coaching (SSC) mindset as developed by Windy Dryden. This is based on a mindset of setting out to do enough in the initial session 'as if' it will be the only one, while aware that subsequent sessions are not precluded[14].

So, I devised a three-stage model as a template for coaching at international education recruitment events:

1. Clarifying of goals for the event
2. Interview preparation
3. Final decisions

Clarifying of goals

This stage potentially lends itself to the Fundamental coaching domain; a model-based, linear coaching approach, which a coach without previous experience of the international education sector could deliver. It requires exploring options and targets for the recruitment event and as such a basic structured coaching model, such as the TO GROW method (see Part 1), could be implemented.

Taking into consideration the limited time available, this stage is about clarifying the end game for candidates, defining success and looking at options for how to go about achieving those aims over the course of the event.

In relation to setting up the goal, the ISMART model[15] can be helpful: Inspiring, Specific, Measurable, Achievable, Relevant and Time bound elements provide an overarching framework. Also remember the AIM SMART goal-setting process and the seven key coaching skills outlined in the Fundamental domain (in Part 1).

Decisive questioning such as 'What are your priorities?' can be effective to ignite dialogue around next career steps or wider holistic themes. If it is possible to engage with coachees before the recruitment event, you can use the visual imagining action tool Polaris (see Part 1 Fundamental domain) as a pre-task to clarify goals prior to coaching and allow progression to the next phase of the model quickly.

Preparation

This stage is focussed on the interview itself, using role play to define key elements of their experience that candidates would like to promote as well as developing their interview technique. Directive coaching approaches can benefit candidates here, such as interview advice for the international education setting. Good preparation coaching necessitates both micro and macro systemic knowledge, in this case, an understanding of what international leaders look for in an interview, drawing on sector knowledge.

Asking empowering questions is a key coaching technique that will enable candidates to practice scenarios, gain confidence and fully cement their interview strategy. Prompts, such as, 'Tell me why you are interested in this role/country?', 'What is it about you that makes you such an effective teacher?' and 'How will you demonstrate your commitment to making a success of living overseas?' can be very effective and closely align to Kolb's experimental reflective model[16], that is, reflecting on previous experiences in preparing for the new. He outlines four areas: Experience (what happened?); Reflect (what was my experience of it?); Conceptualise (Why did it happen) and Plan (What will I do next time?).

Decisions

Perhaps the coachee has received numerous offers and must decide which to accept. It is also possible that a coachee does not receive an offer and is weighing up their next step in light of this disappointment. Bringing together all the elements can make the decision-making stage the most challenging from a coaching perspective, taking into account the multi-dimensional nature of transitions being discussed.

Ideally, the coaching is aligned to a meta-systemic approach[17]. Creating meta-plans can be a beneficial coaching tool at this stage. For example, ask how the decision affects other aspects of their life, or the lives of others affected by what is being considered. The coach at this stage is coaxing the coachee along, holding their interpersonal space lightly, to land at final conclusions of their own accord without inadvertently influencing decisions. In the words of Chinese philosopher Lao Tzu, 'At the centre of your being you have the answer; you know who you are and know what you want.'[18]

This stage correlates with agile coaching considerations and skills; as the coach you need to have the ability to move quickly between coaching modalities. Engaging with non-directive approaches works well, particularly in terms of the coach being detached from the decision-making process from an ethical standpoint.

Asking permission to move into a more directive and mentoring role may also be required: simply ask, 'Would you like to hear what I think about this?'. The core coaching techniques of paraphrasing and summarising once again help to clarify conversations and set potential decisions in context in order to move forward.

Conclusion

International education is fast moving and somewhat transient in nature, so coaching in this setting calls for a multi-dimensional approach including core skills, cultural awareness and strategies to address a plurality of different needs across a broad (systemic) canvas.

Coaching in the setting of a two-day international recruitment event challenges some general coaching assumptions, such as more is better, transformation happens slowly and gradually and an effective coaching relationship takes time to develop[19]. One of my coachees at just such an event, a teaching candidate at a Bangkok international education recruitment fair, substantiates this: 'In a few short minutes, I realised what I hadn't realised in maybe 10 years.'

The context of an international education recruitment event shines a light on the wider coaching discussion around coaching generalists versus the hyperspecialisation. The professed necessity of coaching specialisation forms the core of a vast and well-meaning approach across an array of sectors[20]. Is it necessary to develop a specialisation for coaching at events such as those I have described?

In my opinion a small number of coaching specialists working collaboratively in a 'combination coaching' style could be beneficial for unpicking each stage of the recruitment coaching process. For example, the coach involved in the clarifying of goals could be without sector-specific knowledge, ensuring the detachment required to formulate non-bias goals with the candidate. Then a recruitment coaching expert at the preparation stage explores career decisions and interview technique, before handing over to an expert career coach for the decision stage. However, I concede that this specialist approach might prove difficult to implement in practice due to time and organisational constraints!

The current coaching approach at international education recruitment events is framed around 'expert generalists', able to work in a variety of coaching and mentoring areas and modalities. Such 'contingency coaching' needs to be agile, able to work in a variety of coaching niches, aware of various coaching strategies and their importance at the different stages of a recruitment event.

The concept of more directive coaching approaches – in terms of providing sector- specific insight and mentoring – has its benefits, within ethical guidelines. Perhaps sacrificing a modicum of depth for the breadth that comes with the accumulation of coaching experience in differing contexts can positively impact candidates in these settings[21] and might be seen as the best fit in terms of event logistics.

In my experience, international schoolteachers often possess a pioneer outlook, their interest piqued by the allure of moving to alternative, if not exotic, climes and (potentially) risk-taking with their career direction. Whether generalist or specialist, for coaches to meet the demands of the international teaching community , it will require some challenging of traditional coaching rhetoric and a willingness to be proactive in developing coaching expertise.

References

1 & 2. International Schools Consultancy (2017) International Schools Statistics (available www.iscresearch.com/)

3. Civinini, C. (2019) One in Four Teachers Needed Overseas (www-tes-com.cdn.ampproject.org/c/s/www.tes.com/news/one-four-teachers-needed-overseas-2029?amp)

4. Haywood, S. (2018) Navigating the Agile Leadership Paradox (https://ukicfconference.org.uk/)

5. Christodoulou, D, (2017) Testing the Water Report (available www.lkmco.org/wp-content/uploads/2017/11/Testing-the-Water-Final-Report-WEB.pdf)

6. Black, P. & Wiliam, D. (1998) Inside the Black Box, Raising Standards Through Classroom Assessment, Kappan Classic, US

7. Schön, D. (2017) Learning, Reflection And Change (https://infed.org/mobi/donald-schon-learning-reflection-change/)

8. Bush, T. (2011) Theories of Educational Leadership and Management (4th ed) Sage, UK

9. Whitmore, J. (1992) Coaching for Performance: A Practical Guide to Growing Your Own Skills, Nicholas Brealey, London

10. Morgan, K. (2019) The Coach's Survival Guide, McGraw Hill, US

11. iPEC Coaching (2013) Coach Manual Part 1, iPEC, US

12. Dotlich, D. (2005) in Morgan, H., Harkins, P. & Goldsmith, M. (2005) The Art and Practice of Leadership Coaching, Wiley and Sons, New Jersey, US

13. Morgan, K. (2019) The Coach's Survival Guide, McGraw Hill, US

14. Dryden, W. (2019) Single Session Therapy: 100 Key Points and Techniques, Routledge, UK

15. Campbell, J. & Van Nieuwerburg, C. (2018) The Leader's Guide to Coaching in Schools, Crown Publishing, UK

16. Kolb, D. (1984) Kolb's Learning Styles and Experiential Learning Cycle, (www.simplypsychology.org/learning-kolb.html)

17. Lawrence, P. (2019) Philosophy of Coaching: An International Journal Vol.4, No.2, November 2019

18. Williams, V. (2013) in Wildflower, L .(2013) The hidden history of coaching, McGraw Hill, US

19. Dryden, W. (2019) Single Session Therapy: 100 Key Points and Techniques, Routledge, UK

20 & 21. Epstein, D. (2019) Range: How Generalists Triumph in a Specialized World, Macmillan, US

A Coaching Way of Leading in the Context of International Teacher Training

When leading the establishment of a new International Postgraduate Certificate in Education (PGCEi) at a UK Russell Group university the possibility of implementing a coaching approach presented an opportunity to engage with my passion. This chapter explores and demonstrates a coaching way of leading through a case study of the development of the PGCEi.

Coaching Culture

According to research from a 2017 joint study between the International Coaching Federation (ICF) and The Human Capital Institute (HCI)[1], coaching impacts many talents and organisational outcomes including the improved functioning of teams, increased employee engagement and increased productivity.

Alongside these benefits, I was also looking for a deeper connection in terms of being part of the PGCEi programme development, engaging peoples' strengths and sense of purpose. With this in mind, it was relevant to approach this project from a wider perspective. The concept of growing people alongside developing the PGCEi programme itself appealed to my coaching philosophy. In essence, I wanted to transcend traditional performance management cycles, obligatory institutional training and the sharing of resources to create something more personalised and meaningful.

As we have outlined previously, 'A coaching culture is one where coaching is the predominant style of managing and working together, and where commitment to grow the organisation is embedded in a parallel commitment to grow the people in the organisation.'[2] This idea of value and purpose-based work is very much aligned to the concept of spiritual leadership.

Spiritual Leadership

Spiritual leadership, as defined by Fry[3], comprises values, attitudes and behaviours necessary to intrinsically motivate yourself and others, which entails creating a vision wherby organisational members can experience meaning at work and in life and have a sense that they make a difference. I was intrigued by this: what was the difference we were making by developing an international teacher-training programme? As programme leader had I reflected on the 'Why?', taking into account the needs of all stakeholders, whether students, trainee teachers, schools or PGCEi staff?

Holistic overview

Was there an overarching narrative to be articulated? I found it beneficial to draft initial mission statements through the lens of the different PGCEi stakeholders to further clarify our holistic purpose.

The mission statement applicable to each stakeholder group was:

Children: Helping to educate children worldwide, providing opportunities for children to further themselves and realise their potential.

Trainee teachers: Offering trainee teachers a robust and reflection-driven programme that enables them to impact childrens' education internationally, grow as professionals and as people.

International schools: Supporting international schools' professional development by offering teacher-mentoring training with the aim of further supporting both our trainees and mentors.

PGCEi staff: To establish a high trust culture whereby staff are fully engaged through their areas of expertise with a sense of support, membership and belonging.

Challenges in enacting spiritual leadership

Naturally, there are challenges to implementing spiritual leadership, depending on the setting and individual, team and organisational contexts. This was certainly true in this case.

Vision

The PGCEi is consistently connected with a range of stakeholders university-wide as well as in different educational institutions across four continents. The challenge was to construct a vision for the PGCEi course that also aligned with the wider institutional aims of all programme stakeholders. Aligning these potentially competing elements, whilst also enshrining a coherent programme vision that allowed for meaning, would be difficult to navigate and cement.

Resource

Whilst enacting spiritual leadership through coaching methodology, time and resource should be given to allow people to align with their own individual sense of purpose, meaning and development. A positive example of this has been a colleague using their role in the PGCEi to feed into their Master's studies. Scholarly leave is available to allow this member of staff to pursue their work outside of the institution. Whilst a perk in higher education, I recognise that offering scholarly leave is not standard practice in schools, however.

Performativity culture

A performativity culture, where hard and fast qualitative measurements are consistently valued over 'softer' more transformational approaches, can have an impact on the enactment of spiritual leadership and coaching. Decisions in large organisations can, at times, be financially driven.

Put simply, when culture works against you, it is almost impossible to get anything done[4].

Synergising Spiritual Leadership and Coaching

This is my framework, based on the International Coaching Federation (ICF) Core Competencies for synergising coaching with spiritual leadership, in the context of the PGCEi programme development.

Setting the foundation

- Establishing meeting and training procedures and so setting the culture for the way things are done.
- Spending time with individuals to gain an understanding of their purpose and direction both at work and beyond in order to create synergy and develop a shared vision. This is an ongoing dialogue rather than solely a formal process.

Co-creating the relationship

- Taking time outside of formal meetings to engage with colleagues, establishing trust, intimacy and a sense of belonging.
- Continue to craft opportunities to more fully understand people's purpose and to align accordingly.

Communicating effectively

- Active listening and powerful questioning in meetings and all interactions to ignite conversations, set direction and enhance relationships.
- 'Managing up' to ensure senior leaders are informed of developments and remain supportive.

Cultivating learning and growth

- Creating awareness of operations across all aspects of programme development, designing actions and managing accountability.
- Transferring awareness, skills and knowledge into wider life to achieve and align greater meaning.
- Continue to celebrate individual and team success.

A Paradigm Shift

To fully embrace and enact spiritual leadership through coaching necessitates a paradigm shift to a different way of operating.

The extent to which this coaching way of leading requires an emphasis on applying 'soft' approaches to management and performance indicators is up for discussion. As previously outlined, Legge[5] describes a 'developmental humanism' which treats the employee as a valued asset, proactive rather than passive, engaged not distant, worthy of trust and commitment. Put another way, a 'stakeholder' perspective seeks to more closely align the individual with the organisational mission. This approach recognises that people are thinking, dynamic and interactive beings, not just a static resource waiting to be used[6].

The key issue for institutions moving forward is the potential for further aligning personal and organisational goals. Once employees have been encouraged to pay attention to their progress at work, the organisation must be able to respond to their medium and long-term aspirations[7].

It occurs to me that the purpose of the PGCEi course is simply to provide a portal through which to discover and engage people's spirit, whether trainee teacher, school mentors or university staff.

References

1. (201) Joint study between the International Coaching Federation (ICF) and The Human Capital Institute (HCI), (https://coachingfederation.org/blog/new-research-highlights-millennial-leaders-first-time-managers-need-succeed)

2. Clutterbuck, D. (2018) How to Create a Coaching and Mentoring Culture in Your School, [PowerPoint presentation] Unlocking Potential Conference,

3. Fry, L. (2003) Toward a Theory of Spiritual Leadership, The Leadership Quarterly, US

4. Deal, T .E. & Kennedy, A (1983) in Stoll, L. & Fink, D. (1996) Changing Our Schools, Open University Press, Buckingham, UK

5. Legge, K. (2005) Preview/Postscript for Anniversary Edition from Human Resource Management: Rhetorics and Realities, Basingstoke: Palgrave Macmillan, US, in Whitehead S. (2012) Keele tutor notes, Keele University, UK

6. Martin, J. & Fellenz, M. (2010) in Whitehead, S. (2012) Keele Tutor Notes, Keele University, UK

7. Bratton, J. & Gold, J. (2007 4th ed) Human Resource Management, Theory and Practice, Palgrave Macmillan, US

Part Five

Final Thoughts

Coaching can be a catalyst for educational change, but we need to look for new coaching interpretations for this specific setting, a configuration which looks familiar in education. It requires individuals, teams and organisations to navigate the tension between complexity and simplicity in the coaching approaches discussed in this book.

In education we tend to neglect the transformative in favour of the transactional. There is clarity and certainty in focusing on the transactional and linear, but we also lose a sense of freedom, liberation and mastery that comes from a multi-disciplinary approach. We need to be all ways coaching.

Coaching is about developing self-responsibility. I think we all have a collective responsibility to continue to move coaching forward in education. This necessitates moving on from purely Fundamental to broader Systemic and Transformative approaches, ways of coaching that are more closely aligned to the way our sector operates. It requires a shift in position by us as coaches, moving from the transactional to the transformational with a desire to search deeper into themes. It also requires union across the sector.

As I've described, I believe that a coaching way of teaching can reinvigorate the education sector, through formal, non-formal and informal approaches framed round the three coaching domains. A multi-disciplinary approach will bring the dissimilar closer together and create valuable teaching and learning relationships across age ranges, phases and curriculum.

A coaching way of leading underpins the way we work in education settings, moving towards a more people-centred, unifying approach.

Practitioners at ease with ambiguity and uncertain contexts are potentially more able to improvise in their leadership style, allowing strategy to emerge organically and work. All ways coaching allows leaders to sit comfortably with turbulence and work alongside it.

Coaching is a very personal thing. It grows as you grow. I'm still learning and discovering all the time and I know I'll be all ways coaching for some time to come.

Acknowledgements

With the professional work I undertake I am fortunate enough to be able to visit schools and work with educators all over the world. I would like to thank all the schools, teachers, students, leaders and coaching clients that have helped shape my thoughts on coaching and made me a better person in the process. Thanks to all my podcast guests who continue to inspire me with their stories and expertise.

I would also like to thank the following people who supported me with the writing of this book through overseeing drafts and edits: Chris Seal, Denry Machin, Emma Wilkinson, Karen Smith and Mal Krishnasamy.

A particular mention to Karen Smith who has kept the project on track wonderfully with her proof-reading and general mentoring.

My designer Edd Newson always produces superb work and has done a great job with the cover as well as diagrams throughout.

Thanks to Jennie Chilton for putting up with lots of early morning, weekend and late-night writing.

Lastly, thanks to Andy Buck for planting the seed on a podcast interview and being open enough to publish.